W9-BZN-227

Advance Praise for
The Crowdfunding Revolution

"Thank you for writing the declaration of independence for our industry!"

—Mat Dellorso, WealthForge, Inc.

"*The Crowdfunding Revolution: How to Raise Venture Capital Using Social Media* is the first book in its kind. It should be on the mandatory reading list for everybody active in the industry or for everyone who's planning to be."

—*Crowdfund News*

"We (RocketHub) were honored to contribute quotes, concepts, and our own unique takes on how crowdfunding is changing the world. Now this book is being released to the world—and we recommend it highly to anyone who is fascinated by this new methodology for funding projects and endeavors.... Much thanks to Dan and Kevin for putting these insights and discoveries together in a wonderful read."

—Brian Meece, RocketHub

"Kevin and Dan are onto something. If you want to be part of the next wave to change the world economy, this book is a must read. Both authors combine their own insight but also manage to capture the ideas of all of the major players in the space. It is a smooth read, and the more difficult concepts are broken down into simple pieces. Read this book if you want to catch the next wave!"

—Fred Bryant, founder of WealthForge, Inc.

"I finished your book last night, and it continued to be juicy and very thought provoking right to the end. Thanks."

—Michael Sauvante, Commonwealth Group

"Kevin Lawton and Dan Marom have done a great job at getting really deep into the field of crowdfunding. The book reads like they have had the opportunity to take a look into the future to see the potential of crowdfunding. The book contains an excellent explanation about the concept of crowdfunding and the rules of the game and is a must read for everybody entering the field of crowdfunding!"

—Gijsbert Koren, Douw&Koren
Crowdfunding Consultancy Agency

"This book is a comprehensive introduction to the concept of crowdfunding. The examples (which span across the past, present, and the future!) spice it up well. A must read for anyone interested in the early-stage funding process."

—Mandar Kulkarni, pluggd.in

THE
CROWD-
FUNDING
REVOLUTION

HOW TO RAISE
VENTURE CAPITAL
USING SOCIAL MEDIA

KEVIN LAWTON AND DAN MAROM

New York Chicago San Francisco Lisbon London Madrid Mexico City
Milan New Delhi San Juan Seoul Singapore Sydney Toronto

The *McGraw·Hill* Companies

1 2 3 4 5 6 7 8 9 0 DOC/DOC 1 8 7 6 5 4 3 2

ISBN   978-0-07-179045-1
MHID   0-07-179045-4

e-ISBN   978-0-07-179046-8
e-MHID   0-07-179046-2

We appreciate corrections and feedback (find us at www.thecrowdfundingrevolution.com).

This publication is designed to provide accurate and authoritative information in regard to the subject matter covered. It is sold with the understanding that neither the author nor the publisher is engaged in rendering legal, accounting, securities trading, or other professional services. If legal advice or other expert assistance is required, the services of a competent professional person should be sought.
                    —*From a Declaration of Principles Jointly Adopted by a Committee of the*
                    American Bar Association and a Committee of Publishers and Associations

McGraw-Hill books are available at special quantity discounts to use as premiums and sales promotions or for use in corporate training programs. To contact a representative, please e-mail us at bulksales@mcgraw-hill.com.

This book is printed on acid-free paper.

The bottom line of the human spirit is purpose.
To those who live with purpose.

CONTENTS

INTRODUCTION

Ask not what the world needs. Ask what makes
you come alive, ... then go do it. Because what the
world needs is people who have come alive.
— Howard Thurman

C rowdfunding describes the collective cooperation, attention, and trust by people who network and pool their money
and other resources together, usually via the Internet, to support
efforts initiated by other people or organizations," as defined by
Wikipedia.[1] That's a pretty good start, although the true social
vibrance of crowdfunding is difficult to capture in a definition.
The crowdfunding space is quite diverse and composed of many
niches, and it shares a lot of social networking's energy. Whether
to solicit donations and create a fan base for an around-the-world
sailing adventure, to presell copies of a book, or to finance a start-
up in return for equity, some form of crowdfunding is available.
Just how encompassing crowdfunding is speaks to the enormity of
its potential for economic and social impact. In the same way that
social networking changed how we allocate time, crowdfunding
will change how we allocate capital.

Never before has the human race truly integrated the collective wisdom of our now 7 billion people with mechanisms to allocate capital. Yet well over 2 billion people already use the Internet, and usage penetration is increasing rapidly.[2] Until this moment in our history, capital allocation was largely the province of a relatively small and entrenched minority. Given the lack of available mechanisms to coordinate otherwise and the relatively slower rate of historical change, our systems necessarily coped. But with the exponentially explosive growth of connectivity and complexity via our physical and social technologies, the classical human-to-human networks and centralized planning of capital allocation are folding and becoming increasingly dysfunctional. What are weaknesses of the old methods, especially the sheer scale and volume of information and ideas, are strengths of a new model of funding that has the potential to tap an almost unfathomable collective intelligence to process this collective complexity. Therein lies the immense future of the crowdfunding revolution.

To the more recent generations, thoughts of days without social networking are only a subject of amusement and storytelling. In the same way, future generations will likely grow up with crowdfunding and wonder how venture financing functioned any other way. So many socioeconomic changes that have already taken place were accompanied by fervent disbelief, often from the incumbents. There's no reason to believe that crowdfunding will be any different. In fact, we're seeing the beginning of that. But one has only to look around to see the major shifts enabled by modern technologies. Book publishing, just to pick one, has been radically transformed by the ability to publish electronically. In fact, my coauthor Dan and I live some 7,500 miles (12,000 kilometers) apart, and we have never even physically met. That would have been nearly impossible not so long ago! More broadly, the entire media industry has undertaken systemic change, often begrudgingly integrating with the electronic age of social networking that we live in.

In 1865, a young French sculptor named Frédéric-Auguste Bartholdi went to Versailles, where he had an inspirational conversation with Edouard de Laboulaye, a prominent historian and admirer of the United States. De Laboulaye observed that the first centennial of the United States would occur in just over 10 years, in 1876, and he thought it would a kind gesture if France presented America with a commemorating gift for the occasion. Bartholdi had the inspiration of a giant statue, one that he would spend many years involved with, of a woman called "Liberty Enlightening the World." The statue itself would be paid for by the French people, and the pedestal that it stood on would be financed and built by the Americans.[3]

Years later, Bartholdi founded the Franco-American Union, a group of French and American supporters, to help raise money for the statue. And he recruited Alexandre-Gustave Eiffel (who later designed the Eiffel Tower) for its design work. But as the centennial date approached, the project was behind schedule, and it was difficult to raise the funds to build the statue in France. Bartholdi et al. continued anyway. Then in 1880, they had the idea of holding a "Liberty" lottery. Fortunately, French law permitted lotteries for charitable and artistic causes, and the French government authorized the lottery. Among the prizes were models of the statue. It took time, but the crowdfunding efforts on the French side ultimately succeeded.

On the American side, things were not going well. The U.S. Congress didn't want to provide funding for the pedestal, and neither did New York. As pieces of the statue were built, they were shipped to America, where they were used as tourist attractions to raise money. But that didn't raise enough. In 1883, when the U.S. Congress voted down a new attempt to provide funding for the pedestal, Joseph Pulitzer, publisher of the *New York World*, was outraged. He launched a funding campaign in his newspaper. But at that time his reader base was not very large, and it produced very little in donations. As things broke down, other states began competing for the location of the statue. But as Pulitzer's reader base grew, he made another attempt, and he repeatedly implored readers to donate, appealing to the charity of the masses, no matter how poor. This time, the campaign started producing results. When it was announced that the ship containing the statue's crated parts would leave France, a new wave of donations occurred. Soon, work on the pedestal was restarted. The funding efforts captivated the entire country, money poured in, in however small quantities people could give. The *World*'s circulation exploded, and at one point it enjoyed the honor of being the most widely read newspaper in the Western Hemisphere.[4]

There's a fantastic and historical poster from the American Committee in charge of the construction of the base and pedestal, which solicited donations in the following way: "Every American citizen should feel proud to donate to the *Pedestal Fund* and own a *Model* in token of their subscription and proof of title to ownership in this great work." What's even more intriguing is that the committee used a two-tier "perks" approach: $1 scored you a 6-inch statuette, and for $5 you got a 12-inch statuette.[5]

Sometimes, when you have a dream, it takes an inspired crowd to help make it a reality. We, as a people, feed off others' hard work, vision, energy, and momentum—something that is especially true when the reward systems allow everybody to participate.

According to the late Peter Drucker:

Every few hundred years in Western history there occurs a sharp transformation. . . . Within a few short decades, society rearranges itself—its worldview; its basic values; its social and political structure; its arts; its key institutions. Fifty years later, there is a new world. And the people born then cannot even imagine the world in which their grandparents lived and into which their own parents were born.[6]

This is a book about such a transformation.

Deep and intertwined in our humanity is a need to support and feel involvement in the kinds of projects and companies that we care about. Until the recent crowdfunding phenomenon emerged, our more centralized and intermediated capital formation and funding mechanisms scarcely recognized the social power of crowds that form affinities around any kind of mission. Crowdfunding is a natural systemic response to fill this gap, and it is an expression of our collective human will. It is, perhaps, one of the most powerful developments in our modern-day socioeconomics, and it promises both to transform the capital formation landscape and to offer an avenue for a creative and intellectual rebirth.

Whether funding sports car racers, start-up companies, independent movies, fashion, scientific research, or community projects— crowdfunding is already well under way, changing not only the way that we fund efforts but the way we interact and support them. It is, in the most simplistic terms, social networking meeting venture financing. And a number of people in venture financing are now getting involved in it. There are now 7 billion of us, and over 2 billion of us have Internet access. Never before has there been such potential to bridge the collective creative and productive capacity with capital and other resources that are required to translate that capacity into social and economic activities. Even as exciting is that crowdfunding links funding with the social dynamics and affinity groups that naturally surround efforts that resonate with our many motivations. That alone is enough to cause a monumental shift in the way businesses and organizations operate.

Join us on this intellectual discovery. Part I describes the diminishing function of conventional venture financing mechanisms, vital to an understanding of the emergence and value of crowdfunding. The journey then weaves through the current crowdfunding landscape. And as many readers are interested in the mechanics of crowdfunding campaigns, Part II lays out some of the most comprehensive research and analysis of the campaign to date. And finally, Part III is a visionary look at a powerful new social and economic future, including technological, sociological, and regulatory directions.

Many of you helped shape this journey, and we hope many more will do so along the way. We deeply hope you are inspired and that you become part of what makes crowdfunding's future great.

PART | I

THE ROAD HERE

The road to success is always under construction.
—Lily Tomlin

Chapter | 1

THE RISE OF THE CROWD

If Facebook were a country, it would be the
3rd most populated.
—TechXav

The Group of Seven (G-7), an international organization established to facilitate economic cooperation, dates back to the member nations' summit meetings circa 1975, but it was officially established in 1985, not that long before the commercialized Internet was born.[1] In the ensuing decades after its establishment, a lot has happened on the global economic scene, including the expansion of the group to become the G-20, representing 20 of the world's major economies. But another important trend, at least as profound, has been growing: the number of Internet users in the world has grown to over 2 billion, out of a total population of 7 billion. If we utilize the number of Internet users as a proxy for sizing the available Earthly "crowd," then we have already in essence implicitly formed the Group of 2 Billion (G-2 Billion). And given the current rate of Internet penetration and population growth, in just a few years or so, we may have in just three decades transitioned from the G-7 to the G-7 Billion.

This isn't creative hyperbole. Use of the crowds has disrupted or has begun to disrupt an extraordinary number of business and social activities. Until the more recent crowdfunding trend emerged, many uses of the connected crowd were referred to under the more encompassing rubric of "crowdsourcing," a term coined by Jeff Howe in his 2006 *Wired* magazine article "The Rise of Crowdsourcing."[2] Conceptually, crowdsourcing using the connected crowd has been in use for much longer than the term *crowdsourcing* has existed. Perhaps one of the earliest and most high-impact examples is the free software and open source movements that now power many of the world's websites. In fact, free and open source software development has been ongoing since long before the Commercial Internet Age, back when, as your author can attest to, e-mail had to be addressed through an ugly predetermined routing path (the "bang path" for you cadre).

It's hardly surprising that the earliest adopters of what we now think of as crowdsourcing were technology enthusiasts: technology was much harder to use, and enthusiasts were close enough to the technology to be aware of its potentials. Equally as unsurprising were the motivations of the early adopters, which are perhaps better expressed by asking the contrary "Why wouldn't they?" Human nature has always driven people to seek others with common interests and to commune in those areas of interest, as embodied in the proverbial "Birds of a feather, flock together," the essence of which dates back at least to the Greek philosopher Democritus (circa 460 BC).[3] The latent urge has always been there, and the Internet (even prior to its commercialization) has served to merely open up the playing field to a much larger group. Opening up the playing field it did, as the Internet-enabled open source movement built an ever-increasing momentum and entered the mainstream in the late 1990s and early 2000s, coincidental with the general technology initial public offering (IPO) bubble. It received the most flattering of endorsements any newcomer could hope for by the incumbents, being called a "cancer," "communism," "hype," and all kinds of other terms of validation, especially when emanating from big players who would otherwise not waste their breath. Remember the Ghandi-esque "First they ignore you, then they laugh at you, then they attack you, then you win"? Open source was already in the third phase by then.

Today, Microsoft has a web page dedicated to open source, but at the time it was launched, Microsoft took a very different tone: "We recognize the value of working with others . . . ,"[4] which the company wrote out in a familiar and personalized handwriting style, as if on a chalkboard. Well, we now live in a world in which the power and value in collaboration are much more widely respected.

What's been interesting about the name-calling, across the social networking spectrum from open source to crowdfunding, is that they all got it wrong. A more apropos term might better have been "community-ism" because that's what it is—decentralized, self-determined community clusters woven into the tapestry of the greater whole. Communism, by contrast, is when community is centralized, intermediated, and dictated to by a hierarchical bureaucracy. Or in other words, it uses a power structure that often resembles, at least in spirit, the place where an overwhelming percentage of the name-callers come from.

As the web revolutionized the general population's access to information and to each other, and as it made doing so increasingly easier, opportunity costs dropped. What happened to open source happened similarly to a broader class of crowdsourcing and other forms of accessing the general crowd. Mobile phone penetration exploded, and the phones got smarter including offering access to the web. Innovations in personal computers and their portability continued to accumulate, and personal computers morphed into netbooks, tablets, and other form factors. Mobile data plans, WiFi, Internet terminals at libraries, coffee shops, and airports—and more recently Internet-enabled TVs that have applications much the same as personal computers—all are part of the wave of increasing connectivity that has fueled the crowd. And there is absolutely no mystery in any of this—the power of the crowd is essentially a mathematical inverse function of opportunity costs (including lack of access). Technology and Internet access have changed everything.

Wikipedia is one of the most publicly visible "crown jewel" achievements of crowdsourcing, involving massive and organic orchestration. But behind the scenes, search engines such as Google feed on even more massive and yet implicitly crowdsourced information—the web of intersite references (links) on the Internet. Kiva popularized crowdsourced microlending to entrepreneurs across the globe for the purpose of alleviating poverty. CrowdSPRING and 99designs offer crowdsourced graphic design. Springwise crowdsources business idea spotting. The Google Translator Kit mixes artificial intelligence (AI) and crowdsourced language translation. kaChing and Covestor crowdsource finding investment managers. The pilot Peer To Patent[5] project opens the patent examination process to public participation, and it has been trialed with some successes in the United States, Japan, and Australia. Even in the quant hedge fund industry, there is Algodeal, which allows people to build their own quant strategies on their platform—Algodeal allocates money to the best strategies and lets the algorithm authors share in the profits![6]

A relatively exhaustive list of crowdsourcing efforts would be an enormous undertaking; a shorter list might be one that itemizes the industries which have not been subject to crowdsourcing. On the long list of the industries that have used crowdsourcing are drug discovery, oil and gas research, search for extraterrestrial life, Mars crater analysis, map and traffic information construction, restaurant and movie ratings, T-shirt design, problem solving, executive recruiting, web usability testing, fashion design, news, and photography. And it was only a matter of time: there is now a *crowd conference*,[7] billed as "the world's first conference on the future of distributed work," and a *crowd consortium*.[8] *Many* people and organizations now recognize the value of working with others.

The Dynamic Duo: Social and Physical Technologies

Conceptually, the collective wisdom and power of the crowd dates back to *at least* the days of Plato in ancient Greece, where dialogue was the essence of participative democracy. While a peer-to-peer democracy was effective only in local politics at the time, they didn't exactly have Internet access either. Unfortunately, even though our avenues of communication have increased, dialogic forms of democracy have actually deteriorated, intermediated by decreasingly less representative forms.[9] So politically, we have scarcely even experimented with the collective wisdom, and we seem to be headed in the opposite direction. And yet technologically, we are in just the beginning of what portends to be a quantum leap forward in the collective wisdom of the human race.

In modern times, it seems almost a bit trite to evoke the Internet as a change agent. But there is some stellar work with fascinating observations that suggests we are in nothing short of a revolution. The book *The Wealth of Networks: How Social Production Transforms Markets and Freedom*,[10] written by Yochai Benkler (professor for entrepreneurial legal studies at Harvard Law School), is one of the most thorough, insightful, and articulate masterpieces related to this field. It should be required reading material for every political figure or policy maker. One of Benkler's observations captures the essence of growth in our new Internet-based *complexity economics*:

> The rise of the networked, computer-mediated communications environment has changed this basic fact. The material requirements for effective information production and communication are now owned by numbers of individuals *several orders of magnitude*

larger than the number of owners of the basic means of information production and exchange a mere two decades ago [emphasis mine].

But even beyond indicating changes in scale, Benkler goes further to explain changes to the nature and structure of our economy:

> The removal of the physical constraints on effective information production has made human creativity and the economics of information itself the core structuring facts in the new networked information economy. These have quite different characteristics than coal, steel, and manual human labor, which characterized the industrial economy and structured our basic thinking about economic production for the past century.

Enormous changes to the scale, content, and nature of our modern economy are, alone, enough to warrant the characterization of a "quantum leap" amid our otherwise evolutionary socioeconomic path. But Benkler elaborates something much deeper and more profound—that is, that the patterns in our social wiring have been applied to an expanded role, and they have become very central to the modern economy:

> We merely need to see that the material conditions of production in the networked information economy have changed in ways that increase the relative salience of social sharing and exchange as a modality of economic production. That is, behaviors and motivation patterns familiar to us from social relations generally continue to cohere in their own patterns. What has changed is that now these patterns of behavior have become effective beyond the domains of building social relations of mutual interest and fulfilling our emotional and psychological needs of companionship and mutual recognition. They have come to play a substantial role as modes of motivating, informing, and organizing productive behavior at the very core of the information economy.

In *The Origin of Wealth*, Eric Beinhocker differentiates two types of technologies: physical and social. As he defines, *physical technologies* (PTs) are "methods and designs for transforming matter, energy, and information from one state into another in pursuit of a goal or goals."[11] And *social technologies* (STs) are "methods and designs for organizing people in pursuit of a goal or goals."[12] While the advancements of PTs have and will always be incredibly important, modern advances in STs have been legion and have pervaded many parts of our lives. Facebook, LinkedIn, Twitter, Meetup, Yelp, text messages, cloud computing—these all have strong ST elements, in that they change the way we organize.

Breaking out technologies into these two camps is very useful because it's then quite intuitive to think about much of our recent cultural changes in this Commercial Internet Age in terms of familiar STs. But at a macro level, STs have enabled a powerful phenomenon, a source of the magical powers of the crowd. In Beinhocker's words:

> Once the evolution of STs reached the stage at which large numbers of people could form cooperative networks and had the means for communicating and storing significant amounts of data, human organizations took on a different character—they became capable of emergent computation. Organizations of people have the ability to process information and solve complex problems that individuals cannot process or solve on their own.

Accessing a crowd is not only a way to access more people—the crowd can be much greater than the sum of its parts.

If you were to ask inventors just how radical their inventions are, if they're honest, they'll likely tell you their inventions are actually incremental improvements over, or aggregations of, other inventions. That's mostly been the state of affairs in the history of inventions, as it has for most human achievements, poetically articulated by a statement attributed to Isaac Newton: "If I have seen farther it is because I stand on the shoulders of giants." Given the nature of incremental advancement and the sheer number of potential inventors, it explains why there is quite often parallel "spontaneous inventions" of similar design. And it certainly does not bode well for the efficacy of an intellectual property system in an age of social networking, especially one of patents. But what is truly exciting in this regard is that the natural and perhaps exponential multiplier effect of inventive incrementalism takes on a whole new exponent when the entire crowd is given access. Beinhocker recognizes this almost fractal effect, observing, "One of the most remarkable things about human Physical Technology is how each new invention creates both the possibility of, and the need for, more inventions."[13] One could easily contend that Beinhocker's observation would apply in spades to social technologies.

Affinity Groups

It would be an untenable proposition with any sizable crowd to communicate actively in an every-person-to-every-person fashion. Information flow would quickly overwhelm the participants, wreaking communications havoc and likely subtracting value instead of adding it. While obviously for mostly one-way communications, a large number of people can potentially receive information from a given source (the hub-and-spoke pattern), as soon as there is a material amount of two-way communications, that relationship breaks down rapidly. For a small number of people, of course, a tight every-to-every pattern of communication may suffice.

What's incredible about networked crowds is that they form structural patterns, which arbitrate a living balance between the various participants' needs to actively communicate and connect to other parties. They can be hierarchical or even fractal patterns, each level providing a nexus to the next. But there's nothing saying the structure has to be optimal. It only has to be functional. When it's not reasonably functional, any one member would be inclined to unplug from his or her current part of the overall pattern and presumably plug into a more suitable place. Thus the structure of a crowd tends to be in a dynamic state of continuous rebalancing.

To help visualize the awesome complexity and beauty of an interconnected crowd, look at Figure 1.1, which is a fantastic graphic that was created by Chris Ward from his research studies on social networking and prediction markets at the University of Utah's School of Business.[14] The figure depicts a social network graph from a project on trader behavior in an online prediction market. A picture is worth a thousand interconnected words.

Figure 1.1 A Social Network Graph from a Project on Trader Behavior in an Online Prediction Market

Source: Chris Ward, http://www.spurstream.com/blog/, accessed in 2010.

One of the most important components in the structure of a networked crowd is formed by an *affinity group*, which can be loosely defined as a group of people with similar interests or motivations. They are in part responsible for various pieces of information getting traction by and exposure to the larger crowd and also for maintaining the higher collective intelligence of the crowd (as opposed to central command structures that tend to dumb people down). The role of affinity groups was very elegantly articulated by Benkler in *The Wealth of Networks*:

> Filtering, accreditation, synthesis, and salience are created through a system of peer review by information affinity groups, topical or interest based. These groups filter the observations and opinions of an enormous range of people, and transmit those that pass local peer review to broader groups and ultimately to the polity more broadly, without recourse to market-based points of control over the information flow. Intense interest and engagement by small groups that share common concerns, rather than lowest-common-denominator interest in wide groups that are largely alienated from each other, is what draws attention to statements and makes them more visible.

Affinity groups can be durable and static in constitution. But they can also be characterized more as dynamical systems, reformulating in real time.

When the right balance of adaptability, credibility, and other mechanisms are combined, affinity groups represent the soul of scalability and efficacy of utilizing crowds. And this is not limited to the day-to-day activities we usually think of as befitting of crowdsourcing. Another such area of promise, for example, is in their application to humanitarian operations, especially during times of crises. Jonathan Gosier, in his blog post "Crowdsourcing and Chaos Theory,"[15] discusses issues and directions in using the crowd for humanitarian operations, with the aim of enhancing decision making with dynamic inputs from the crowd. As he points out, a number of humanitarian groups operate like football teams, with prescribed plans of action. However, this type of planning often breaks down:

> I'm of the belief that humanitarian operations reflect dynamical systems. Political variables, organization structure, the people selected to run programs—these are variables that, from the outset, affect everything that organization will try to do because they aren't "constant." They change over time in reaction to things changing around them. Most organizations try to contain "the butterfly effect" by favoring deterministic methodologies.

As is Gosier's point, crowdsourcing isn't really crowdsourcing without using the crowd, and one needs to use the crowd in a very dynamic system. Thus, he proposes using inputs from the crowd to buffer against dynamic change.

Although he doesn't propose any specific solutions, he touches on one of the most critical aspects of the power (and future) of crowdsourcing—notably, how the crowd collectively validates information (for better or worse), calling this phenomena "folksonomic triage," derived from *folksonomy* ("people defined") and *triage* ("condition-based decisions"). One of the problems with such folksonomic triage is that herding occurs around small early bits of information, which can have very negative effects if the information is incorrect or fraudulent.

This is where, I believe, we are only in the beginnings of our potentials in understanding and properly using affinity groups to rapidly identify, assess, and otherwise influence crowdsourced decision making. Affinity groups can be thought of as amplifiers, so tomorrow's crowdsourcing mechanisms can help amplify accuracy and truth by offering mechanisms to assess credibility, timeliness, and possession of what's called *local information* (information that is held by only a few), and they can facilitate these assessments in near or actual real time across an arbitrary set of participants for a given event or outcome.

It's important to note that a person who otherwise serves as an excellent affinity group member for one group (or crisis event) may well not have the proper local information to act as an amplifier for a similar group (or event) if the local information requirements are different. This difference can be simply a change in physical location, but it can relate to almost anything else including political affiliation, time zone, language, and culture. It is my belief that discovering an effective means to facilitate rapid affinity group assessment is the province of tomorrow's crown achievement in realizing the power of crowdsourcing, and it will likely be a differentiator in the winning crowdsourcing (and specifically crowdfunding) platforms.

Participation and the New Pro-sumer Class

David Johnson, then a visiting professor at the New York Law School, wrote in his piece about virtual companies: "The marketplace speaks the language of price. Traditional companies speak the language of obedience. Peer production speaks the language of love."[16] It's a grave mistake to think in terms of a clear producer-consumer divide. This is an age of a substantially more engaged crowd, both in terms of defining what they consume and how they consume it. These are sentiments echoed by the words of Joanna Shields, vice president and managing director for Facebook Europe, Middle East, and Africa (EMEA): "The most important word in the Internet world today is not *search*. It's *share*."[17]

Besides contributing to *Wikipedia* and open source, we as a collective do web mashups ("a web page or application that uses and combines data, presentation, or functionality from two or more sources to create new services"[18]), remix YouTube videos, review restaurants, share our photos for others to incorporate into their web posting, post our favorite news items to the likes of Digg and Slashdot, rate and comment on those same news items, share links prolifically, create blog posts and send tweets, create our own game mazes, answer questions on Quora, review books on Amazon. com, and of course use our phones to cast votes for *American Idol* contestants. Whether we participate by creating a mini-opus page on *Wikipedia* or simply push the "Like" button on Facebook, we arc nearly all pro-sumers now (a blend of the words *producers* and *consumers*).

Along with the evolution of the pro-sumers came the *pro-ams*—"amateurs who work to professional standards,"[19] as the authors of the book *The Pro-Am Revolution* described them. These are essentially a new and third class of people—those with talents and knowledge on a par with or sometimes exceeding the professional class but who appear more as the pro-sumer class. Many quality bloggers fit this category, as do many photographers and independent filmmakers. This trend isn't at all surprising. Given enough people with valuable talents and knowledge, all that was necessary to enable them to express themselves was a lowering of the opportunity costs of doing so. And the development of increasingly easy to use and more powerful Internet and social networking tools enabled precisely that.

The Response to the Loss of Social Capital

In the book *Bowling Alone: The Collapse and Revival of American Community*,[20] Robert Putnam describes how we have become "increasingly disconnected from family, friends, neighbors, and our democratic structures," and he warns that "our stock of social capital—the very fabric of our connections with each other, has plummeted, impoverishing our lives and communities." In this context, it becomes clearer that the rise of the crowd is not purely a response to new opportunities. It is, in many ways, a revival of our social needs to interact and be part of something larger—our intrinsic hunger for a sense of community.

For whatever suburbanization, the television, the change in women's roles, and even access to computers did to diminish social capital, there is a corresponding promise in the utilization of the crowd to revive forms of community, such as when it is used as an effective means of facilitating local activities: "America has civicly reinvented itself before—approximately 100 years ago at the turn of the last century." It's critical to comprehend the magnitude of the societal imbalance that has occurred in that duration of time in order to contemplate the natural counterforce that is looking for an outlet. And then one must realize that social networking, crowdsourcing, and crowdfunding are smack in the middle of that outlet. This isn't a fad, it's not a bubble, and it's not a mania. This is our culture.

The New Crowd-ployment Paradigm

The question "Where do you work?" embodies an until-now very entrenched employment paradigm, one in which we are generally associated with a single company. But along with the diffusion of the consumer-producer and professional-amateur boundaries comes a similar effect on the employer-employee relationship. Or as Benkler states: "The emergence of radically decentralized, non-market production provides a new outlet for the attenuation of the constrained and constraining roles of employees and consumers."[21]

As opportunities increase for us to avail ourselves to exposure as pro-sumers and pro-ams, and as crowdsourcing and crowdfunding give us opportunities for employment in a style that is closer to contract work, it is increasingly possible for us to survive financially as *crowd-ployees* (people who gain their income largely from crowdsourced activities). Writers, for example, can write and sell e-books, but they can work in their downtimes as editors for other writers' books, facilitated through a crowdsourced editing site that uses reputation-based referrals. The same writers may even recycle some of their income into investments in independent films, perhaps participating in the writing or editing of the scripts. In this model, it's not even clear what an employer is. The flip side of this equation for companies is that they can tap the crowd to perform an increasing number of their tasks and, even more important, to make an increasing number of their *decisions*. Certainly, smaller agile companies will be created that use the crowds more extensively, right from the beginning. This will and is changing the nature of the employer-employee paradigm and the way we work now and in the future. But it will also make for some thorny intellectual property (IP) entanglement issues—another reason to contemplate a refactoring of the IP system we have in place today.

The Crowd-poration

From the point of view of open source development, it's easy to understand how living, dynamic groups can thrive, even while spanning the globe and encountering a certain amount of churn in the body of developers. There isn't necessarily a sense of a geographic epicenter, or in corporate terms, a headquarters. Neither is there generally a "board of directors" that periodically convenes, takes notes, and makes big decisions. Rather, decisions are made continually, and the power structure is codified not by contractual documents but by whatever dynamic forms are in use. But open source is just one example of a growing class of virtual organizations that organize mostly or completely via social and other forms of networking. Unfortunately, this model has not really been available to profit-seeking organizations who organize in a similar fashion. Traditionally, an organization is generally forced to fit into the physical-centric corporate structure, with all its paperwork filings, meetings, and physical address requirements.

At least that was the case until June 6, 2008, in the state of Vermont, in the United States. Pioneered by David Johnson (then a visiting professor at the New York Law School) and others, Vermont passed laws that allow companies to form and operate entirely online. As the associated wiki[22] states: "There is no need for paper-based filings, in person (or even synchronous) annual meetings, or a physical address for the company. . . . In other words, you can create a wiki for profit!" That solicited some interesting news titles, including "Vermont Wants to Be the 'Delaware of the Net,'"[23] a nod to Delaware for being the go-to state for incorporation in the United States for many physical companies due to Delaware's corporation-friendly laws, fees, and taxation.

That could make Vermont, at least in the United States, a designation for crowdsourcing and perhaps crowdfunding. It will be interesting to see where this leads.

Chapter | 2

THE DECLINE OF
ESTABLISHED FINANCING

*Even in decline, a virtuous man increases the beauty of his
behavior. A burning stick, though turned to the ground,
has its flame drawn upwards.*

—Saskya Pandita

According to a 2003 report, Morgan Stanley studied the prospects of start-ups over the prior 22-year span, including every single technology IPO in North America. The results: only 1 in 20 start-ups made it to an IPO, and only 1 in 20 of those companies actually created shareholder value thereafter.[1] Anecdotally, a similar trend can be seen in start-up "exits" (that is, start-ups being sold) via mergers and acquisitions. From those results come some very important observations. Even dating back to a period starting circa 1980, the lack of value in start-ups symptomatically indicated an unhealthy Venture Capital (VC) industry—unhealthy not purely because of the number of failures but also because of the lack of sustainable value in the ones that were associated as successes.

While much ado has been made in the VC industry about performance concerns due to the lack of an IPO window, the study gives a clearer picture why. Initial public offerings weren't just an important form of VC liquidity. They were in many ways used as a dumping ground for low-value start-ups, sold in part to the public. However one interprets the dismal post-IPO odds of shareholder value creation, it's hard to interpret the Securities and Exchange Commission (SEC) regulations that drove private start-up investments largely into the hands of the professional and the wealthy as having had a positive effect for the general investor.

Given Venture Capital's dependence on a healthy IPO market for providing an important liquidity option, one's first inclination might be that the VC market is inherently cyclical with respect to the broader economic and equity market conditions, and thus it will eventually return to its previous glory. But the reality is that there are many secular forces that, combined, are disrupting and further transforming the start-up creation and financing landscapes forever. Many of those same forces, while disruptive to classic VC financing, are concurrently feeding and giving rise to a new form of venture financing that we call *crowdfunding*. And what Venture Capital is to start-ups, Hollywood is to movies, and so on.

These are deeply entrenched, opaque, and centralized complexes with relatively few participants, operating based on largely antiquated business models formulated long before the advent of the Internet and even longer before the social networking movement. But it's very important to note that while crowdfunding embraces many of the more current socioeconomic trends, it does not represent a modular or symmetric "drop-in" replacement for classic venture financing. Rather, because crowdfunding is potentially a much more organic, transparent, and decentralized phenomenon, reaching an extremely broad audience, the boundaries of its transformative effects will be hard to define, yet extremely pervasive. This is the first time in our history that the world at large has or will become part of the financing of new ventures of all types. Given the scale of the socioeconomic changes we've already encountered from new forms of connectivity, a deeply profound set of changes awaits. This is the crowdfunding revolution.

The Rate of Change

Let's look at some of the forces at work, disrupting classical financing mechanisms, the first of which is monumentally important: the rate of change. Change is everywhere, and it's picking up steam across the board, whether embodied in physical technology or social technology or financial complexity. A great way to fully appreciate an increasing rate of change is via a quick review of the history of "ages" in the world. The Stone Age lasted about 2 *million* years, while the Bronze Age lasted about 2 *thousand* years. The Commercial Internet Age is less than 20 years old, but the Twitter Age is only a few years old. That's the time compression resulting from an exponentially increasing rate of change, illustrated in Figure 2.1.

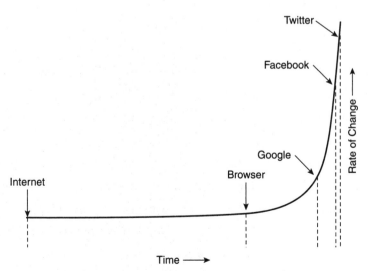

Figure 2.1 The Time Compression Resulting from an Exponentially Increasing Rate of Change

We could perhaps refer to each of these periods of time as a *technology generation*. This is in analogy to the concept of a *familial generation* (the average time between a mother's first offspring and her daughter's first offspring[2]), which is about 25 years in the United States. Using this analogy, one can see that many years ago things moved so slowly that a single technology generation spanned potentially numerous familial generations. One could actually pass down knowledge about technology from generation to generation, and it would still be relevant. Wow, have things changed! Sometime around the advent of the Commercial Internet Age, the compression of technology generations made them smaller than familial generations, to the point where there can be many within a single familial generation. We now live in a period of time perhaps best described as the "Change Age." And that has and will have profound implications for venture financing.

The Durability of Expertise

In a day when technology generations were, let's say, 20 years, one could build up quite a nice body of expertise. But what exactly is an "expert" when a given technology has a lifetime of 3 years? Although various contemporaneous technologies have different lifetimes, some much longer than others, how can any small group of financiers claim that they have more expertise over the others in a field with a high rate of change? Without expertise, then what exactly are the advantages offered by various incumbent financing outfits? The answers to these questions speak to the change that has been disrupting venture financing in the last decades. In high rate-of-change environments, the irony is that "experts" (or at least the people delivering the most value) are likely not to be those from the previous generation.

Perhaps this is behind James Surowiecki's observation in *The Wisdom of Crowds:* "Similarly, there is very little correlation between experts' self-assessment and their performance. Knowing and knowing that you know are apparently two very different skills."[3] This almost has to be the case. Without knowing how long any particular technology will last and to get enough utility out of any one expertise, human nature will drive most people to the end of that technology's short life, when it becomes too late to establish oneself as an expert for the next already under-way technology. This is a key reason why it's now more important than ever to tap into a much larger collective crowd to find and vet opportunities. Some interesting ways to do this are discussed later.

A Multidisciplinary World

Imagine if innovation were a balloon, representing the generational lifespan of technology. If we were to squeeze the balloon across one dimension, it would naturally tend to bulge out in another. That bulging is nature's way of diverting the energy from the squeeze to somewhere else, in this case into the cross-disciplinary nature of today's big ideas. Not only is there a cross-disciplinary trend in many new ventures but it was logically inevitable. In a 2009 Technology Trends panel discussion at MIT, the panelists independently created a list of their "Top 5 Technology Trends for 2015." One of the panelists, Anand Deshpande, made this trend forecast: "Multidisciplinary products. Many different sciences intersecting with technology to produce interesting new products."[4] But it's not just MIT panelists recognizing this trend. A *TechCrunch* article came out entitled "It's Official-ish: Teens Totally Admire Steve Jobs More Than Mark Zuckerberg."[5] One of the major reasons for this trend: "31 percent cited success in multiple fields as what makes an entrepreneur stand out." Apparently, if you want to understand our cross-disciplinary future, just ask the younger crowd.

But it just makes sense that the compression of change in any one dimension has limits, given that there are only 24 hours in a day, a lot of which are occupied by some other important activities such as sleeping, eating, conversation, and watching *South Park*.[6] So the "whitespace" for innovation, the unexplored territory, tends to exist at the intersection of multiple disciplines. And who advances such multidisciplinary innovations? According to the findings of *The Medici Effect*,[7] one of the most important books relevant to innovation ever written, these innovators are rarely ever "experts" but rather people who apply knowledge from one or more fields to another. By contrast, what we have traditionally thought of as an expert is someone who has focused intensely in *one* field.

Where we're headed, our sense of expertise needs to be much more multidimensional. And because the right mix is harder to find or identify, it is increasingly important to reach out to a larger base of people to find it. That also foretells a change in the structure of companies and other organizations.

Market Time Compression

Over the years, the Venture Capital industry's strategy has morphed from that of a slow follower to a fast follower. Venture capitalists used to have the luxury of waiting until more established markets arose, at which point they would then fund start-ups to compete within those markets. As the technological rate of change advanced, however, the VCs got quicker to fund "me-too" plays (that is, fast following). But to this day VCs are still lacking in their visionary ability to fund first movers. And this has been killing them. A shrinking technological generation means a compressed market lifetime and a quicker requisite time-to-market. For a market that lasts 20 years, there's an argument for waiting a few years. But if a market lasts for only 3 years, delaying entry into the market by 1 year could be terminal.

Historically, being a first mover, while conferring a level of bragging rights, has also typically meant that a lot of resources were expended paving a road that someone else got to drive over. It was like the proverbial pioneers with arrows in their back. That sentiment has not been quick to die off in the VC industry, yet change marches on. As the rate of change increases, the lost opportunity cost of waiting to invest increases. By the time venture capitalists are in, it's often too late. Gone is the day of the follower, replaced with the day of the market maker.

But as market time compression marches onward, another shift is to be anticipated. Whereas a given start-up used to focus on creating one valuable good or service—call this a *building block*—the future entails the funding and creation of multiple building blocks to materialize a new market. When taken together, the building blocks are part of a larger offering. Further compression will drive even more real-time selection of building blocks (therefore, it may be imperative to fund competing building blocks and let the chips fall as they may) as part of an integration story for start-ups, shredding whatever is left of predetermined plans. Versatility will be key going forward, and just as much for the financiers. The only way it would seem this will work is if the people funding the process are part of the process. The best way to find those funders is in the crowd.

Capital Efficiency and the Rolling Close

During the question-and-answer (Q&A) session at a VC-panel-based entrepreneurial event, I asked the panel what was the last big innovation in Venture Capital financing in, say, the last 10 or 20 years. This seemed like a fair question directed at an industry that purportedly facilitates the creation of a lot of innovative companies. There was a lengthy, if not embarrassing moment of silence. After grappling to come up with an answer, one of the panelists finally admitted that the Venture Capital industry is not really very innovative. That may explain why some of the VC companies are still housed in digs on Sand Hill Road in Menlo, California, where office space can cost as much as 8 or 10 times that of cheaper available space. Nevertheless, the VC industry mercilessly chimes on about driving capital efficiency into their portfolio start-ups.

There is in any case, a very real trend of starting companies on very small initial funds. Cloud computing, open source tools, crowdsourcing, outsourcing—there are many mechanisms to get something off the ground with lesser money. As a number of venture capitalists have said in private, over 90 percent of start-ups that need servers use Amazon EC2 from day 1—the cloud computing server rental model. The effect that the lower financial barrier to starting companies has had on Venture Capital is simple to explain. Venture Capital derives its value from providing money (the other golden rule: "He who has the gold, rules"), so if start-ups require less capital to get started, Venture Capital has less value. And thus, the venture capitalists went off chasing larger and later-stage deals.

Compounding the diminishing VC leverage, another trend is taking hold: the *rolling close*. The very lumpy and discrete round-of-funding model has been incrementally replaced by the rolling close, whereby start-ups take money from investors incrementally until they feel they have enough. This was a change adopted and explained by Y Combinator's Paul Graham.[8] This change creates advantages for the entrepreneur "because it requires less reliance on a lead investor, takes less time out of product development, and gives investors less room to drag things along or collude."[9] In short, this is better for the entrepreneurs because it more closely matches funding to their needs. It's not surprising that an entrepreneur turned angel investor would be quicker to adopt this new funding model, as articulated by Paul Graham in a *TechCrunch* video interview: "If you want to be an investor ahead of your time, just figure out how founders would like you to behave and start doing that now."[10]

All this translates to less VC leverage. To get good returns and at the same time invest enough money "to move the needle," venture capitalists have to be really good at investing in early-phase start-ups, *and* they have to invest in enough of them to make it worth their while. They'll be pushing harder and harder against multiple compression waves. Ultimately, what is needed is to tap into the collective crowd to solve this; small teams of people just will not be able to synthesize enough information.

Macroeconomic Sensitivity

A cruel irony about Venture Capital, not just to start-ups but to the job growth engine that stems from smaller companies, is that it is beholden to the macrofinancial climate, including the IPO market and the equity markets in general. Many of the limited partners (LPs) that invest in Venture Capital funds have approximately 6 percent statutory caps on the amount of risk capital they deploy, some of which goes into VC. When other asset classes reprice downward (as equities do by the millisecond), it's easy for the slow-to-reprice VC assets to make the relative ratio of risk capital exceed the caps. The short of it is, the LPs won't make good on capital calls, and they certainly aren't inclined to chip in to new funds. Not only does that leave the VC fund short on capital but it also tends to force VCs to nurse their existing portfolios instead of funding new start-ups.

Lack of a healthy IPO window (or "dumping ground," as was previously explained) creates an environment in which existing start-ups compete for private capital, and the lack of a liquidity option mathematically eats away at the LP returns by way of the time-value-of-money effect of VC fees. These kinds of macrosensitivities conspire to make VC very cyclical in nature, which is quite a shame. Just when economies need future investments the most to spur the next round of economic activity, Venture Capital is the least effective (and incidentally, many of the world's fortunes and innovations were made during downturns). These are yet more reasons that any promising new funding models need to be decentralized and spread out to the many.

The Start-Ups' Response

A common mantra in the start-up culture used to be "execute, execute, execute," as if any given start-up was a laser-beam focused automaton on a rigid and completely knowable linear path from creation to market penetration. This wasn't just a consequence of a finite amount of money from the latest round of funding from Venture Capital. It was driven by the rigidity of the deal terms and milestones set early on and the potentials of an equity dilution death spiral when things didn't go according to plan. But the rigid execution mentality was on an inevitable collision course with an advancing rate of change, and it has proven to be a better indicator of outmoded thinking and naiveté than it is an indicator of potential success. If the world around a start-up is in constant flux, then so too needs to be a start-up's direction. While changing directions used to be a near-death experience for start-ups, now it's common fare.

"Pivot" is an often necessary element of the new "execute." A *pivot* expresses the ability to change directions quickly, but it does not necessarily mean a holistically different direction. In fact, it often describes a change to an adjacent direction. In an MIT talk, Eric Ries well summarized the new role of the pivot as an essential part of the evolution of a start-up when he stated: "The difference between a successful and an unsuccessful start-up is the number of pivots a start-up makes before it dies."[11] Similarly, Robert

Scoble observed: "Some things that startups that aren't run well do: You don't change direction fast enough. Every startup should be looking at its direction every month or so."[12] And from Paul Graham, who has developed a considerable amount of data points from his own incubator efforts at Y Combinator: "In the average Y Combinator startup, I'd guess 70 percent of the idea is new at the end of the first three months."[13] The new and improved mantra might be better expressed as "pivot, pivot, pivot." Change needs to be an intrinsic part of any project.

This divergence between the old-school linear "execute" mentality still held by a number of financiers and the new "pivot" model exposes something perhaps best referred to as "the execution paradox." Those start-ups that are adapting and changing as they should are not "executing" against their prescribed milestones. Consequently, they may well get eaten up by Venture Capital and all of the classic downside deal terms. However, those start-ups that are *not* adapting and changing as they should may have the appearance of "executing." In a high rate-of-change environment, such start-ups are statistically likely to be failing. This paradox is one created out of problems with perception and inability to dynamically evaluate a given start-up's prospects—the expected outcome of a limited set of people overseeing a new venture in such a complex and fast moving macroenvironment.

The Venture Capital Industry's Response

Absent the technology investment bubble of the late 1990s to the upside, or the global financial crisis to the downside, Venture Capital would have followed an inevitable path that led it to the same place the industry has largely gone: it would have moved toward the later-term financing of deals. Why? Because the VC industry has largely been ill equipped to handle the high and ever-advancing rate of change. Chasing later-term deals is, in some ways, an attempt at chasing history—going after less volatile deals that the market has "validated" and that appear to be less subject to many further changes. To the astute financial types, this is also a form of *backwardation*, whereby relatively longer-term risk is valued less than closer-term risk.

Of course, chasing "de-risked" deals comes with some major ramifications, even for the limited partners who invest in Venture Capital. For one, there are fewer deals of this kind to go around, and they are known to a much broader audience; thus there is more intense competition for the deals. More demand and less supply drive the prices that VCs have to pay up to get in, and thus lesser returns follow. This also explains why some of the big "brand name" firms still do reasonably well, as getting premium access to these known deals can be more of a game of the perceived value that those brand name firms offer, generally in the "Rolodex department."

There is another way that Venture Capital can chase a lower rate of change, and that is to invest in "greenfield" sectors that have relatively longer development cycles (less compression) but that are generally capitally intensive in their financing needs. Clean technology is one prime example, but there are a number of others. All of this is not to say there aren't some great economic and ecological effects of these funding developments. The important point is that it was destined to happen and predictable, and it has had some profound ramifications for the state of affairs in funding early-phase start-ups—notably that obtaining such funding has become extremely difficult. And also important is that VC industry returns will continue to decay, until a new funding paradigm emerges. In fact, many in the industry believe half of the current VC firms will die off in the new few years.

But why is it that VC firms cannot adapt to this change quick enough? One way to look at this question is to simply restate it in a broader sense: "Why can't any small group of people adapt to change quickly enough?" Well, if that small group is focused on navigating through the sea of change within a very narrow universe, then perhaps the group has a fighting chance. But even then, the group will have to contend with the cross-disciplinary trend that has been building, something that is discussed in more detail later. For any VC firm's partners, or for that matter any panel of "experts," there is some bad news forthcoming: they have been outmoded. Not only has the durability of expertise depreciated, but also, combined with the necessity to be very cross-disciplinary, the future will require one to be extremely adaptable and have multidimensional intellect and exposure.

In a later part of the book, new VC funding models that are integrative with respect to crowdfunding are presented—funding models that thrive on change instead of fighting against it. It's highly recommended that those in the funding industry consider some of these new ways of cooperating with the crowd not because it's some fad but because it's predictably necessary due to supply and demand. The supply of people who are extremely adaptable, have relevant multidimensional intellect, and can synthesize tremendous amounts of systemic change on a regular basis are sure to shrink on a relative basis as the complexity of the world increases and the rate of change advances. Yet the collective wisdom of the crowd happily grows with all of these factors. Our recent decades represent a boundary period for venture finance, sort of a modern-day Cretaceous–Tertiary (dinosaur) extinction event resulting from asteroid impact.

The Market Sizing Fallacy

Imagine a start-up executing through the pivot-pivot-pivot, seat-of-their-pants business reality. That's the high rate-of-change environment in which start-ups have to live in these days. Let's say that they're creating a new market, and after a number of pivots and other adjustments to the real-time world around them, they succeed in creating a nice new market for themselves. What are the odds that they could have accurately sized their market, a priori? The answer is something like "from slim to none." Facebook, one of the hottest properties online, was initially created as a way for college students to connect. Now it has more than 900 million users, a fact that nobody doing "market sizing" would have imagined in the early days. Perhaps for some markets, where the aim is to disrupt the incumbents by displacing them, it's a more tenable proposition to approximate market size. But even then, the world is changing rapidly around the incumbency as well. Market sizing has become one of the biggest fallacies, promulgated largely by the types of people who don't actually operate near the battle lines.

In reality, a much more tenable strategy is to make quicker decisions and to "fail fast" rather than to "fast follow." Let the markets decide. And who knows the market better than the market itself? Funding tomorrow's new ventures will involve tapping the crowd for both the investment decisions and the de-investment decisions. And speaking of "de-investments," killing off loser plays (or the inability to do so) is even more prone to emotional and "saving-face" attachment issues, and it is often decoupled from the realities of the market further than initial investments decisions are.

The Base of the Funding Pyramid

Life would be a lot simpler if the *funding pyramid*—the shape depicting the fewer later-term deals at the top and many more earlier-term deals at the bottom—were truly triangular in shape! But the reality is that the width of the pyramid diagram is not linear in progression. Rather, it increases exponentially in the direction of the bottom. This exponential shape reflects the natural culling

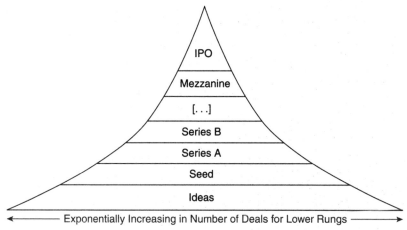

Figure 2.2   The Funding Pyramid

process that occurs as a project goes from the perhaps tens or even hundreds of millions of ideas out there, down to the number of start-ups that meet their ultimate funding objectives, and it is illustrated in Figure 2.2 (not to scale, obviously).

Many ideas or projects die off before each next stage; an enormous number of ideas never go anywhere (as well, many shouldn't). In a world with increasing complexity and change, the opportunities for ideas is also growing, and thus the base of the exponential funding pyramid is also expanding rapidly. But almost paradoxically, in the face of this increasing scale, the incumbent mechanisms for financing start-ups increasingly falter. There are many more powerful new ideas, but the existing system cannot sort through the torrent at the base of the pyramid to find them. What would our economic situation look like if we *could* efficiently sort through and locate good ideas? If the thought occurs in your mind that tapping the collective wisdom of the crowds must be part of the answer, then you're reading the right book!

Chapter | 3

THE DECLINE
OF OUTLIER
IDENTIFICATION

The real voyage of discovery consists not in seeking
new landscapes, but in having new eyes.
— Marcel Proust

We used to live in a much more hierarchical and class-based society. Whether individuals were literate, whether they had a degree, where they got their degree from, how they dressed, whom they socialized with—these weren't just accomplishments. They were social signatures of where the individuals came from and how they lived in the hierarchical and social food chains. In short, these things defined an individual's *status*. Ingrained in human nature is a continuous need to make rapid-fire assessments about other people's abilities. In the past this ranking wasn't done for convenience. It was downright necessary, given a population bigger than the number of people any one person could know well.

So we developed shortcuts—means to quickly assess other people. In a day when there was a strong correlation between status and education (and even more so, literacy), assessing a person's status was a logical and preferred shortcut for predicting his or her ability to perform complex and skilled tasks. Of course in the present day, many people have an education, and even at the graduate degree levels (for example, MBAs), it seems universities are minting new ones for "a dime a dozen," and some of these graduates have a dubious grasp of the modern-day business climate.

But using class as a shortcut has never really left us, especially in the financial world. A number of people in finance have admitted that when filtering résumés, they apply a first-order screen that allows through only those candidates from a few elite academic institutions; the rest are literally wasting their time applying. Now, no generalization works across the whole of any industry, but a lot of VC firms have a similar class filter built in. And many just can't get enough of an entrepreneur with the "right" degree from the "right" college. When the VC firms find such candidates, they seem to be induced into an almost euphoric state. It would be hard to blame them if such a simple filter actually worked. But unfortunately, it doesn't. And it hasn't, for quite some time.

One of the best books ever written about Venture Capital, *Outliers*, never mentions either start-ups or Venture Capital. Well, really it wasn't at all written about Venture Capital, but it's more relevant than almost any other book that ever was. Malcolm Gladwell reveals an interesting study of the performance of coming from an elite college, measured in terms of one's probability of going on to win a Nobel Prize in Medicine or a Nobel Prize in Chemistry.[1] The colleges where the prize winners came from were as varied as the results are striking: using the brand name of a college would not be much of a predictor. Equally as revealing is Gladwell's observation: "We've seen that extraordinary achievement is less about talent than it is about opportunity."[2] In many cases that opportunity was strongly related to being at the right place at the right time in history. Well, the right time is now, and the right place, at least in part, is on the Internet.

Speaking of college degrees, see if you recognize any of the following people who dropped out of some level of college degree program: Bill Gates and Paul Allen (Microsoft); Larry Ellison (Oracle), Sergey Brin and Larry Page (Google); Michael Dell (Dell); Mark Zuckerberg (Facebook); and Steve Jobs (Apple). These people represent a hearty percentage of the American economy. But we shouldn't stop there. Have you heard of James Cameron and Steven Spielberg? Also dropouts, as were the founders of Kodak, Polaroid, Disney, Ford, Learjet, Bank of America, Whole Foods, Jet Blue, Domino's, Dunkin' Donuts, Wendy's, McDonald's, Kentucky Fried Chicken, NBC, Holiday Inn, *and* the people lending their images to the U.S. pennies, quarters, and one-, five-, twenty-, one hundred–, and one thousand–dollar bills!!![3]

In the absence of an alternative, using the college component of status has been slow to die, however long it has been feeble as an indicator or first-order filter. But the preceding list of dropouts debunks another myth of the Venture Capital world: the lucky charm of the superstar entrepreneurs who have a "win" under their belt. Well, maybe some of them do go on to win again, but apparently from the list, if you could pick only one filter, perhaps selecting for dropouts would be a better one. Anyway, four out of five of America's richest people and the people behind many of the world's greatest inventions would have positively matched your dropout filter.

Two factors that were found to be actually significant in *Outliers* were building enough domain experience (at least 10,000 hours' worth) and being at the right place at the right time. Of course, given the cross-disciplinary trend and rapidity of change in the system, identifying outliers will become more complex. In a lot of ways, what the entire incumbent financing industries are up against stems from their mechanisms of finding outliers. Many of these mechanisms (for example, college brand name, past wins) aren't working anymore (and haven't for some time).

Perhaps even important, any alternative filters will also fail if the main modality of networking is diminutive in scale. As *complexity economics* would have it, even though there are many more opportunities every day, there is an even greater amount of *noise* to sort through. Finding and funding tomorrow's outliers (that is, "black swans" in Nicholas Taleb's terminology[4]) requires an ever-expanding reach into an increasingly more complex set of interconnectivities. Small sample sizes are the enemy of finding outliers in complex systems. Likely, clever financiers will find some equally clever new filtering algorithms, but what's clear is that those algorithms will have to be applied to a much broader reach.

And thus, tight-knit networking circles have to give way, at least in part, to utilizing more modern forms such as social networking. The scalability of classic human-centric networks has hit the skids. Fortunately, while the Internet has to a large degree exacerbated this problem, it also holds many potential solutions. We live in the age where billions of people use the Internet, and social networking has become part of our lives, whether we are using Facebook, Twitter, LinkedIn, Foursquare, Blippy, Quora, YouTube, blogging, or something else. The irony is that many individuals who have created big social networking presences have a bigger Rolodex file than many financiers—that is, they do if they aspire to be connected to the next set of outliers. And with the hyperawareness and immersion that come from using these modern tools, many individuals in the crowd have a much better chance of screening and picking the best and most interesting new projects.

Curation: The New Leadership

In the past, leadership was often assigned to those who used political power and currency to extract the most value from others. But going forward, the currency and political influence earned by leaders are gained from adding the most value to the lives of others. The artifice of strong-handed corporate and bureaucratic dictation is giving way to more real and beneficial forms of leadership. It's not just in the blogosphere or in start-up identification that we're seeing this trend. It's happening in nearly every category one looks at.

For example, let's take travel. When booking fun and interesting things to do, our choices were often confined by deals made by travel agencies or by whatever local commercial services were offered. Today, we can find or offer personalized tours, lessons, and other activities through Tripod,[5] "the place to request what you want for your trip and get offers direct from locals to make it happen." It's possible that on your next art tour, the tour will be curated by aspiring artists, and hopefully they won't robotically repeat from a set of memorized cue cards. A similar, albeit early trend can be seen with bookstores. Rather than walking into a typical bookstore in which the selection, categorization, and presentation of the books leaves little room for the personal touch (except perhaps in a smallish section of employee picks), today you can become a member of OurShelves,[6] founded by book maven Kristina Kearns, who has read many of the books which you'll find there. OurShelves is a curated lending library, currently tucked away in the back of an antiques shop in the Mission District, San Francisco. If you were to take either a literary tour of San Francisco or a tour of "the Mission," curated by a Tripbod, they may well take you to visit OurShelves.

Even entire communities are curating their own communities, in an encouraging trend away from dysfunctional bureaucratic planning. Take Rotterdam, for instance. Its 2012 "I Make Rotterdam" project focuses on an area that used to be the bustling town center but now is "dominated by large-scale infrastructure, traffic, and rear facades of buildings."[7] In an effort to "use unconventional means to enliven the area rapidly by creating pedestrian connections and reinforce existing programs," the project team set a precedent by initiating a crowdfunding campaign to fund the building of a wooden pedestrian bridge dubbed the Luchtsingel. The span of the bridge is 350 meters, requiring 17,000 planks, and contributors can kick in from €25 (one plank) to €1,250 (an entire bridge section) and personalize "their" planks with inscriptions. Even more ambitious is the body of thought, if not the movement, behind The Enabling City,[8] which provides a toolkit and holistic outline for interactive community planning and open government.

And of course, crowdfunding platforms were quick to recognize the role of curation, some of them creating special pages for curating parties and banners to let the crowd know which projects were curated. Indiegogo was one of the earlier to this game. The organization had strong partnerships with both the San Francisco Film Society since 2008 and Fractured Atlas (a national community of artists and art organizations) since 2009, but it offered official curation by way of "Partner Pages" in early 2011.[9] Just after, Kickstarted announced its "Curated Pages."[10]

A number of the top blog sites have more traffic than do old-world news empires. To get an idea where we're headed, imagine that dynamic applied to venture finance.

Chapter | 4

THE EMERGENCE OF
EARLY FINANCING

When patterns are broken, new worlds emerge.
—Tuli Kupferberg

It's not as if the entire ecosystem hasn't recognized the dichotomy of the incumbent financing cohort's deteriorating ability to serve innovation, just as the modern complexity economy is exponentially driving potentials of innovation. As in all complex systems in disequilibrium, natural forces and interactions arise that push the system toward a more balanced state. In terms of the early financing of innovation, that push has been manifested in a fairly recent proliferation of mechanisms focused on the early start-up or project phase.

Have you noticed that recent, incubator-style funding mechanisms are popping up everywhere like weeds? In some ways, they were popularized by the likes of Y Combinator,[1] founded in 2005 by Paul Graham and others. But many others have picked up on the theme of organizing around funding and the creation of early-stage start-ups that need generally small amounts of capital

(Y Combinator rarely makes investments over $20,000). Stanford students even created their own start-up accelerator, SSE Labs,[2] modeled after Y Combinator, although it takes no equity positions in the start-ups it facilitates.

In the United States alone, it seems a new incubator is announced at least once a week. This is an important trend to note because it arises for many of the reasons that we've discussed, including the increasing velocity of innovation and scalability issues surrounding the old financing system's handling of the torrent of early-phase ideas. Without much in the way of serious options for equity-focused crowdfunding projects, incubators have been an extremely important solution to a shared problem set. They are, in a sense, cousins to crowdfunding. However, it's pretty easy to see, for a number of reasons that we'll discuss along the way, that the family is about to get much tighter. Let's first have a look at some of the issues with the incubator-style funding mechanisms going forward. This is not at all meant to discredit the nurturing and guidance that some incubators give. Rather, it's that we believe they will morph and become closer to the crowd.

The first issue with incubators is their narrow window into the collective wisdom of the crowd, which arises necessarily from their general constraint to a geographic locality combined with the partitioning of the collective attention span by the sheer number of incubators. Earlier in the game, one could have made the argument that this would work in localities where all the right pieces of the puzzle lived. But remember that these are the new cross-disciplinary times. It's not just that many pieces of the puzzle are more geographically dispersed than ever before. It's that the outlier pieces which complete the most powerful puzzles live in some completely arbitrary places. Building a model that depends on a relatively smaller and smaller cross-section of the collective wisdom is a recipe much like that with which the Venture Capital community has baked for the last couple decades.

As will be discussed in Chapter 10 on prediction markets, the power of crowds is not just gaining access to the best ideas. It is also very much about utilizing the collective wisdom as a sorting and leading-indicator mechanism, which then allows for scalability. And scalability is where other early-phase funding models go to die. Dispersing and partitioning the crowd by the boundaries imposed by today's incubators is quite unnatural and antithetical to utilizing the true power of the crowd. For the short term, incubators and other seed-stage-only funding mechanisms are absolutely necessary because there really hasn't been anything else better. But this is something that can be ameliorated by integration with crowdfunding dynamics—a topic discussed herein.

A second issue that is extremely important to understand is that funding models which focus on seed-only financing can easily get outleveraged by the downstream financiers. All but the obvious ones (where the market has "spoken" loudly already) can get "hung out to dry" when it comes time to raise more money. It's not enough to merely facilitate initial funding; that doesn't in any way guarantee future funding (provided funding is deserved). These are points well made by one of the most vocal voices shaking up the Venture Capital industry, Georges van Hoegaerden from the Venture Company,[3] who argues for a VC model that funds start-ups from start to finish (a monolithic funding strategy).

A superior model is one that facilitates a more continual "rolling close" and offers exposure to a much larger audience (the general crowd), essentially one that offers better funding continuity because it ensures exposure continuity. Perhaps the brand name incubators get this to an extent by way of naturally attracting more players, but this is something that will likely diffuse as the incubator space populates like the Tribbles on *Star Trek*.[4] As an aside, due to the Tribble-like proliferation, there is occasional chatter in the media about a "bubble" in seed financing. Well, the entirety of all funding mechanisms is only supplying a tiny fraction of the demand for innovation capital. This isn't remotely a bubble. It's merely a natural systemic response. Rather than thinking of this as a trend that will bubble up and then retreat, it's more logical that this space will morph and coalesce with other crowd-friendly mechanisms that solve the limited reach and collective attention diffusion problems. But its essence can grow monumentally from here, if nothing else, based purely on the mechanics of supply and demand—something that is currently desperately out of balance.

And a third, and very economically important, issue relating to the current incubator model is that it's generally set up to handle non-capital-intensive funding needs. While it may be the case that commoditization of many technological components has lowered the barrier to entry for many mobile application and online site start-ups, there is a bevy of high-impact ideas that require a significant amount of capital, right from the seed stage. Said another way, there is a huge chunk of global gross domestic product (GDP) that is never created because there is no great way for those ideas to get funded, including incubators. To change this, cooperative, hybridized models need to be implemented, to get the big money running with the same herd as the smaller investors. Use of the greater crowds will stoke this phenomenon, especially given the prediction markets (we'll discuss this later) and affinity grouping dynamics that validate ideas and serve a type of filtering function. There is absolutely no reason, given the right implementation, that tomorrow's crowd-enhanced funding model can't launch the next megacompanies. Many such related ideas are forthcoming in this book.

One of the promising by-products of the last few years of early-phase funding has been what one might call the *open sourcing of deal contracts*. The earlier phase comes with some additional scaling issues, including the legal costs and related human resources spent navigating and negotiating through deal terms. It just doesn't make much sense for a venture taking only a smallish amount of money to expend a considerable amount of the raised funds on the legal contractual process. As well, a number of complex deal terms don't well suit early companies. What's been desperately needed is a standardization and simplification of contracts, so that the process can be streamlined and the contracts can more likely be equitable to the entrepreneurs. Fortunately, a number of fairly recent efforts have emerged to serve these needs.

In September 2007, Ted Wang, an attorney at Fenwick & West, wrote an op-ed piece on the *VentureBeat* called "Reinventing the Series A"[5] that outlines similar issues. In the piece, he volunteered to work with others on solutions. In August 2008, start-up incubator Y Combinator published a set of standardized legal documents that start-ups can use when raising angel rounds of funding.[6] And in February 2010, Ted Wang's efforts produced a separate set of stream-lined seed contract documents,[7] which many investors signed on to using, including the relatively new VC firm Andreessen Horowitz.

This new development bodes well not only for entrepreneurs in general but also for what it enables going forward. Certainly, taking away friction and inefficiencies from the innovation process will help facilitate the creation of more innovation. But also, as funding innovation moves toward the logical direction of utilizing a broader and more collective source of funds, for example, crowdfunding, it enables a more point-and-click-style mechanism for creating deal terms. And that's a very important component in the scalability that any large-scale funding mechanism will have to possess.

Chapter | 5

THE RISE OF CROWDFUNDING

Even countries with few resources and incompetent
governments did reasonably well if they had strong,
well-developed Social Technologies.
—Eric Beinhocker

On October 1, 2010, the Blender Foundation[1] released *Sintel*,[2] an independently produced, animated science-fiction fantasy short film. *Sintel* follows Blender's other short animation film projects: *Elephant's Dream* (2005), *Big Buck Bunny* (2007), and *Yo Frankie!* (2008). In the days of outsized budget movies, *Sintel* was quite a monumental achievement, and not just because of its stunning animation created using the Blender 3D open source content pipeline. It was released as open source, downloadable for free in a number of formats, with separately downloadable subtitles in English, Spanish, French, and five other languages. The total budget for *Sintel*? About $550,000, its production involving a team of up to 14 people working full time.[3] And it was partially crowdfunded.

If you enjoyed the spoof *Star Wreck*,[4] then you may also be following the latest project, *Iron Sky*,[5] by the same independent filmmakers. It's a dark sci-fi comedy, with plenty of computer graphics imagery (CGI), and had a budget of about 6.9 million euros. The *Iron Sky* project pushed the envelope of indie filmmaking, utilizing a hybrid financing model that combines traditional film funding channels and crowdfunding (fans buy "war bonds"; conflict is part of the film's theme) and engages the fans throughout the process. And these are people who know how to engage—their previous Internet hit *Star Wreck* has reached over 8 million viewers. Building on that success, *Iron Sky* was as an international coproduction with bigger name actors and targeted a worldwide theatrical release in 2012.

But then came the technology start-ups. Eric Migicovsky was a 25-year-old Silicon Valley transplant from Vancouver. Like many entrepreneurs, Migicovsky had a product idea inspired from his own life. Being a cyclist, he wanted a smartwatch that would intelligently connect to his smartphone and provide information such as who is calling, GPS location, or messages from friends. This, as it would become clear, was a product idea that resonated with many people, for many uses above and beyond cycling. And it was one that his company translated into the design for the "Pebble" watch. But as is often the case for products with potential, his attempts to raise venture funding for the manufacturing phase failed. So Migicovsky turned to crowdfunding, and he started his Kickstarter campaign ("Pebble: E-Paper Watch for iPhone and Android") on April 11, 2012, with a stated funding goal of $100,000.[6]

Before critics had time to spell-check their hit pieces, dispelling the "myth" of technology crowdfunding, funding for the Pebble passed its funding goal in two hours! A veritable funding rocket, Pebble passed $1 million within a day, and it continued on to breach $10 million within about a month, when on May 13 it was decided to declare the Pebble "sold out." At that point, approximately

69,000 backers had essentially preordered 85,000 Pebble smartwatches. And in classic "fast-follow" fashion, the VCs then began chasing Migicovsky.[7]

How crowdfunding has changed since its first known citation by Michael Sullivan, on August 12, 2006.[8] Crowdfunding is growing up quickly, and in some areas, it is integrating and hybridizing with more conventional financing methods. That's not to diminish the role of crowdfunding in offering complete financing for less expensive indie operations. But what it does highlight is the importance crowdfunding offers to bigger investors as a market validation mechanism. For agile investors, crowdfunding isn't their problem. It's a solution for identifying viable opportunities that are fan and market validated. The operative word is "agile."

If one were to interpolate the cost of *Sintel* to a full-length production, it would be similar to that of *Iron Sky*, on the order of $10 million. By contrast, while Hollywood producers are contemplating how they can sync intellectual property strings to keep their financing complex alive and asking how they "could keep making $200 million movies like *King Kong* without super strong copyright regulations?,"[9] a whole ecosystem of agile players is quickly evolving, with an associated and implicit message: that was the wrong question to ask. What's as telling is that from attending and networking at a recent Kickstarter meetup, there was quite a growing excitement over the potentials of crowdfunding's allowing projects to get "recognized by bigger players." Even for lower-budget projects seeking all of their initial funding goals through crowdfunding, the thought of a bigger future is on a lot of people's minds! Note to Hollywood types: keep a crowdfunding dashboard active on your desktop at all times.

The *Sintel* and *Iron Sky* cases above share a common theme that is echoed throughout the entire crowdfunding ecosystem, at least by those who have invested time and energy in it. Success in a crowdfunded project is built over longer periods of time, and it is the subject of continuous hard work and genuine engagement with the fan base. Many have argued that crowdfunding requires even more of these elements. The Blender Foundation, for example, was officially founded in 2002, and it has built an amazing community around its open source 3D content creation flow, and as we mentioned earlier, it has released a number of short films to demonstrate and evolve its functionality. The *Iron Sky* creators worked on various forms of *Star Wreck* beginning in the 1990s. Or as its visual effects man, Samuli Torssonen, put it:

> Fan/community funding is not an easy way out. We didn't come out of nowhere. We've been building our Internet community and visibility since 1999, with *Star Wreck*. You have to invest a lot of time and energy to win the trust of the Internet audience. The only way to do that is to deliver good quality. Mediocre stuff just won't cut it.[10]

While there will likely always be a few outlier cases of rapid funding without much history, from our survey, the reality for most projects is well characterized by Torssonen's statement. And in case you thought the Pebble watch "came out of nowhere," note that the team had been working on smartwatches for about four years prior and it included an industrial designer who, as the CEO said in an interview, "really killed it,"[11] which of course is the highest of compliments in familiar-speak. A "killer" design and years of technology prototyping went into what would become the Kickstarter pitch, as did the idea of making the "World's best watch." Repeatedly, this trend can be seen, when looking behind the scenes into what appears to the press as "overnight sensations" but that are really cases of real value offered to and recognized by a massive amount of people. In business, this is called "pent-up demand," but sometimes the press (apparently when short on time for research) calls it a "fad."

Movies and technology are only two hot categories within crowd-funding. Food was the third most popular category on Kickstarter, and it had a much higher funding success rate (56 percent) than the average of all projects (47 percent) according to a report.[12] We are infatuated with food and beverage. Food is social, it can be creative and imaginative, and it often comes with a rich story. What's more, there are often a lot of underserved special-needs food categories. So it's not so surprising to see food-oriented projects use crowdfunding for their designs to create almost anything including camel cheese, microbrew beer, a bicycle that churns butter, gluten-free ice cream sandwiches, cupcakes, sustainably raised prosciutto, an online cooking show, a local organic block party, organic dog biscuits, urban agriculture "farm-boxes," a community olive press, city biocentric composting equipment, an urban farm, and a wood-fired bakery.

One of the more community-focused efforts in the food space was the Farm Lot 59 project, which received its funding goal of $10,000 on Kickstarter to develop an urban one-acre biodynamic and organic minifarm. It's a nonprofit organization of people characterized by "We are an accumulation of people living and working in the city of Long Beach, California. We are farmers, gardeners, tree-huggers, chefs, writers, parents, teachers, artists, bakers, and community leaders."[13] Farm Lot 59's goal is to also serve as an educational resource for the Long Beach community, a place where children and their parents can come and learn about urban farming and the Earth's ecosystem, and to create some local green jobs. It's hard to argue that these activities represent anything other than people who want to offer something, funded by people who want those things. And in many cases, a sense of community, involvement, and employment come welcomely attached.

While some folks are busy crowdfunding indie movies and sustainably raised prosciutto, fashion designers are crowdfunding their fashion lines through Catwalk Genius. Race car drivers and golf stars are crowdfunding their "personality securitization" on ThrillCapital. Bands are crowdfunding their next album on Indiegogo and RocketHub. The Japanese firm Music Securities[14] is securitizing media plays using crowdfunding. And wine making is being crowdfunded on Crushpad. New start-ups are being crowd-funded on WealthForge in the United States, WiSEED in France, CrowdAboutNow and Symbid in the Netherlands, and Crowdcube in the United Kingdom. Existing revenue companies are crowd-funding nondilutive debt on Cofundit in Switzerland. Real estate buyers are crowdfunding "shared equity ownership" on PRIMARQ. People in the United Kingdom are crowdfunding loans on Zopa. And the list goes on. In the social ventures dimension, there's 33needs,[15] which has the goal of crowdfunding ventures that solve the world's biggest needs. Hyperlocal crowdfunding is provided by LuckyAnt, Smallknot, and ioby ("in our back yard").

There's even now a crowdfunding diligence company: CrowdCheck. And while many Western countries are cutting their research budgets, the Open Genius Project,[16] located in Italy, has promised to crowdfund research projects, as does SciFund and PetriDish. Asia opened its first crowdfunding site: ToGather.Asia. The Greek platform StartersFund was created among the smolder-ing ashes of a country previously known as the "cradle of democ-racy." Adding a whole new exciting dimension in crowdfunding, the SoKap platform offers a way to crowdfund such that funders get rights to media distribution within a particular geographic territory. If there's a crowd need, it seems there's a way to crowdfund it.

The year 2012 became a pivotal year for crowdfunding. Just after an acquisition of Spot.Us,[17] which had provided crowdfund-ing for freelance journalists for three years prior, 2012 was ushered in by Tom Foremski's post, "Are VCs Abandoning Seed Funding? Report Shows Massive 48 Percent Dive in One Year."[18] That did nothing but seemingly spur on crowdfunding, which made MIT's *Technology Review*'s top 10 emerging technologies list.[19] A quick look at Google Trends for "crowdfunding" supports MIT's trend analysis.[20] When Howard Leonhardt announced his campaign for governor of California 2014, he came out in huge favor of crowdfunding.[21] In April 2012, President Obama signed the Jumpstart Our Business Startups (JOBS) Act, which had among other things, language to legalize crowdfunding. And crowdfunding conferences started to sprout up everywhere. Kickstarter announced in February 2012 that it expected to provide more funding to the arts than the National Endowment for the Arts.[22] And of course, like many popularized technologies such as hard drive storage, network bandwidth, and 3D video, crowdfunding entered the adult content realm, with the introduction of offbeatr[23] and GoGoFantasy.[24]

At the Edge of Chaos

To an outside observer or someone first entering the crowdfunding domain, it probably looks a bit like the "Wild West," an expression we have here in the United States to describe the western part of the country in its nineteenth-century, relatively untamed history. It's not that the observer would be completely wrong; modern crowdfunding is in a very early and noticeably dynamic state. And quite honestly, some of the crowdfunding sites could use some work. But there's a critical point and distinction to make here, and it relates to what is referred to in various math, science, economic, biology, and social fields, called "the edge of chaos." Simply put, the edge of chaos is the notion of a region near the threshold between order and chaos. There's an intuitive way to explain the value near the edge of chaos. If a system is too structured, its very structure prevents it from being very innovative. If a system is too chaotic, its chaos prevents it from being productive. The "sweet spot" of innovation is right at the threshold, and that's the edge of chaos. And that's also thought to be where nature is at its most adaptable place. To achieve the optimum, one must push right up to the edge, and by the way, that's *way* beyond where big corporations generally live today. Rather, many live in the zone that is over the edge of the cliff of usefulness, where they have recently come to be known as "too big to fail."

Although many issues still need to be shaken out in crowdfunding, there's something far more important to recognize. By enabling the collective wisdom to express itself, we are allowing a return back to the optimal place where the system best thrives—right at the edge. Regulation, of course, will attempt to hold it back to being overly structured, and thus it will be less innovative.

In the book *The Future of Work*,[25] Thomas Malone describes a pattern that plays out repeatedly in the history of human civilization. People organize themselves into small bands of decentralized autonomy, which then go on to become larger, more hierarchical groups governed by centralized forces. These groups then finally become larger groups in place but with decision making becoming more decentralized. The book is really a relevant work in its entirety, but it's especially interesting to note how Malone characterizes decentralization in layman's terms: "the participation of people in making the decisions that matter to them." It may seem like the Wild West, but what is occurring is a very natural cycle, and we shouldn't endeavor to truly tame this frontier!

Do It With Others (DIWO)

Since the 1950s, the expression "do it yourself" (DIY) has been all the rage. The gist of the DIY movement is to be able to build, repair, or modify things without experts or professionals.[26] The DIY mindset is one of the key spirits in true enthusiasts, and it is certainly key in the "maker" crowd. For a number of tasks, doing it yourself yields the self-satisfaction of accomplishing things, and that's really all that's needed. But for many others, if you think about it, it's kind of a bummer doing something completely on your own. Fortunately, with the advent of the Internet came the ability to be more easily connect with others who enjoy the DIY spirit for whatever one likes doing.

Whether you're building a contraption to prevent pesky ground squirrels from meddling with your garden, tricking out your camera body with a new attachment, or installing a mod chip in your hot rod, why not find someone else interested in the same? And thus the DIWO movement was born.

Crowdfunding is very much a kindred spirit of DIWO. People in the crowd tend to invest in projects to which they have an emotional and social attraction. Some people make fantasy investments; others want to feel the proximity to a cause they respect. And some investors are friends and family, and they invest because they know the entrepreneur well and want to support him or her. In fact, this latter group is of utmost importance to many crowdfunding initiatives. According to Brian Meece of RocketHub, typically 95 percent of contributions in the creative space come from first- and second-level friends' circles. It's this group that establishes a "trust signal" to the next wave of investors. Without this signal, few get much further.

Ultimately, only a few projects get sufficient momentum to "go viral," and in those cases, 70 to 80 percent or more of the contributions come from strangers. Generally, artists leverage their past works and their existing trust circle "base" to get funding for their projects. As Danae Ringelmann of Indiegogo explains: "No community generally equals no funding." To secure funding, one needs to come to the table with a decent "anchor audience" and do some "moving and shaking" thereafter. An irony here is that while many outsiders fret over fraud in crowdfunding, many insiders fret over just how hard it is to get strangers to contribute money!

And while passion and affinity are major drivers, let's not forget the rewards. For those crowdfunding platforms and projects that return monetary rewards, that speaks for itself. But many current crowdfunding projects offer only perks (especially due to regulatory issues discussed further herein). Because it has often lacked the ability to return financial rewards, creative project crowdfunding became creative with offering rewards. Besides the obvious of receiving the finished goods under funding (CDs, DVDs, books, and so on), funding fans get things like mentions in the credits, appearances in movies, signed posters, discounts, limited edition goodies, funder-only updates, studio visits, and so on. In crowdfunding, those who fund are VIPs. And it's well accepted and quite common that those who fund even more, get even more VIP treatment, via tiered levels of perks (remember, it worked for the Statue of Liberty[27]). But perks aren't just a gratuity. Those who fund are VIPs also because they're part of a project's marketing department, sending out blasts to their Facebook friends and Twitter followers. These VIPs are possibly the catalysts to getting to the next tier of funders. Perhaps they answer questions, invest their time, or even do some design work. *And*, they are a project's most loyal consumers. The DIWO movement is also an important new business mentality.

Of course, as with any social dynamic, there are always a few who don't hold up their end of the bargain. We're only at the beginning of the modern-day crowdfunding movement, so it will be interesting to see what mechanisms develop to punish those that don't produce. It's human nature to demand as such, so one can easily anticipate that we'll see mechanisms arise as soon as there are enough problems to make it socially worthwhile. PirateMyFilm, very much a pioneering platform for crowdfunding media, warns its citizens: "Any producer who fails to live up to their dividend paying responsibility can be voted out of the community and forced to 'walk the plank.'"[28] It's not surprising to see this admonition come first from PirateMyFilm because it's a product of Max Keiser, one of the industry's most visionary people in crowdfunding and the former CEO and cofounder of the Hollywood Stock Exchange, inventor of the Virtual Specialist technology, and the host of the hugely popular *Keiser Report*. At any rate, this presages what is to come in the social norms that underlie crowdfunding.

Critical Mass

While new crowdfunding sites were emerging across the globe, it was hard not to notice an abundance of them in the Netherlands. This stirred up a little fascination, as the discovery of the factors involved might provide insights into what could be done to further ignite crowdfunding as a socioeconomic driver. This is a subject that we fully encourage others to advance because it has no small impact on the future competitiveness of any country or region, vis-à-vis others that have a deeper adoption of crowdfunding. But the following are some salient observations that we can offer.

On the obvious side, crowdfunding is a form of Internet-based social networking, and so it would follow that having a highly connected population with a culturally endemic Internet habit would be a key ingredient. Certainly, the Netherlands would fit this description. According to the Internet World Stats website,[29] an older report showed that "the Netherlands has a small but advanced telecom market. In March 2005, Internet, broadband, and mobile penetration were all far ahead of the EU average." And equally as impressive: "The Dutch have adopted mobile phones enthusiastically. Mobile penetration breached 100 percent in 2005, and annual growth remains at a respectable 16 percent."

If nothing else, the Netherlands received a nice head start in network connectivity, which would then help explain its citizens' cultural proclivity for social networking—they have, relatively speaking, the largest number of LinkedIn users worldwide and Twitter users in Europe, and Dutch topics are quite often trending topics on Twitter, according to Gijsbert Koren of the Dutch crowdfunding site *CrowdAboutNow*.[30] But according to Internet penetration data from the World Bank,[31] also high on the connectivity list are Denmark, Finland, Iceland, Norway, and Sweden. Incidentally, Finland was home to Linus Torvalds, the key protagonist of Linux. And Linux and the greater open source movement that it helped enable, have been perhaps the biggest and most involved crowd-sourcing efforts of the human race.

While connectivity and social networking habits look to be major ingredients, the recipe is likely more complex. And it's not the case that the Dutch regulatory environment is much more amenable—crowdfunding doesn't fit into current regulation there either. In talking with people involved in crowdfunding, we were able to divine other important parts of the recipe, listed in a condensed format below. Special thanks go to Gijsbert Koren for his excellent synthesis and insights:

1. There is high Internet penetration and usage.
2. "Higher income per-capita results in financial opportunities for the adoption of new technologies." It helps to have "people who could miss some of their money; who just put their money into something for fun." This point shouldn't serve to dissuade those in countries with lower per-capita incomes. For the cases in which investors are allowed to be foreign or for those in which investors are local and using crowdfunding to prebuy what they need to buy anyway, crowdfunding can have a monumental impact. Any resulting marginal improvement in the local economy would then feed further growth of crowdfunding. So one could think of crowdfunding in low per-capita regions as having even more relative importance.
3. Lack of capital from investors and banks creates the need for another funding avenue.
4. "Stimulating entrepreneurship by education, business games, and incubators has been a trend in the Netherlands since five to six years. Crowdfunding is a possible add-on to this trend."

5. "The *uncertainty avoidance* (Geert Hofstede's *cultural dimensions*) in the Netherlands is quite low, which suggests we accept new innovations. Other countries with a low uncertainty avoidance: United Kingdom, Scandinavia, United States, Singapore, Hong Kong, Malaysia, China, India, and African countries."

If those factors constitute the fuel, then all one would need for a fire is the spark. And that spark in the Netherlands seems to have come from SellaBand, launched in August 2006. SellaBand allows musical artists to crowdfund from their fans and from the entire SellaBand community, in order to record a professional album. It also allows the recording industry to crowdfund projects for their own artists. In Koren's words, "SellaBand started in the Netherlands and is an important inspiration and quite well known amongst young people in the Netherlands. When I'm talking to founders of other crowdfunding platforms in the Netherlands, they were all (without any exception) inspired by SellaBand."

The New Ritual, the New Status

If you're over at an acquaintance's place, you may find that he or she has some magazines strategically fanned out on the coffee table and handpicked books prominently displayed at eye level on the bookshelf. Socially, we tend to convey our rituals, like our reading proclivities, to others as a form of status. And well, some people just like to convey status for vanity's sake. Crowdfunding, explains Brian Meece of crowdfunding for creatives site RocketHub, is a "new ritual." It takes time for people to adjust to it, as a new part of their daily lives, but it then becomes part of their identity. Recognizing this, RocketHub and other sites provide "badges" that can be used on various social networking sites to convey this identity, much the way people do with the magazines that they (allegedly) read.

As crowdfunding's popularity rises, it will become increasingly more popular to view people's funding affinities, along with all the other tidbits of their lives (both offline and online) to assess their personal character—and of course, to find like-minded people. It's worth keeping in mind that many people originally thought Twitter would never get any traction. It's good that not only the crowdfunding ecosystem recognizes a new ritual but that the whole social networking scene also recognizes it. It may be the case, soon enough, that people won't have much luck on dating sites unless their profile includes some crowdfunding of causes interesting to the suitor.

Rivers Without Cascades

Let's say you're on vacation, looking for a nice place to dine, and you find a nice little cluster of restaurants. In the absence of any particular recommendations, perhaps as a first screening, you cruise the menu listed outside of each restaurant. And then after finding one that suits your fancy, if you're like many people, you have a look inside to see if anybody's eating there already (or maybe you do this first). Let's say there are just enough diners inside to give you confidence about your experience. You have become part of an *information cascade*. The next people with similar circumstances are even slightly more likely to make the same choice—after all, you just added to the apparent business of the restaurant, increasing the *confidence signal* to the next wave.

This phenomenon goes far to explain why restaurants tend to seat the first wave of diners closer to the street windows, presenting a more busy appearance to casual prospects. Using information from earlier sources in the cascade wouldn't be such a bad thing to do if, in the restaurant example, you knew the people inside were mostly locals. But how do you know they're not all tourists? How do you know they're not kitchen staff holding down some tables until the "pump is primed"? Perhaps they are people who were enticed by the attractive hostess offering "free dessert" with their meal.

Many people, when first introduced to the concept of crowdfunding, have an almost visceral response to the concerns of information cascades and other forms of *groupthink* maladies that can result from mass forms of social imitation. And yet a number of them find a very comforting solution to the above dilemma, which is to whip out their smartphones and look up the restaurant's rating in real time on Yelp. They are implicitly trusting the power of larger virtual crowds, over the small physical crowd they can see with their own eyes. So important have the review sites become that various new restaurants and bars have special "soft opens" when the key reviewers are invited, to make sure that everything is "just right" before the real "hard open." And a number of passionate reviewers have called out bogus reviews, created by the restaurants themselves. Never underestimate the power of passion in affinity groups.

Another form of groupthink phenomena, often called the "Keynesian beauty contest," is driven more by each new participant's desire to anticipate what the others will do and then to act accordingly. A classic example of this is embodied in investment strategies. While investors may well look at the fundamentals of a given public company and macroindicators to see where the economic direction is heading, ultimately investing is largely a game of understanding what the others will do next. In short, this occurs when participants are expressing their anticipation of others, not their own passion and beliefs.

And of course, it's quite possible to have the scenario where people are bidding with their passion and beliefs and those beliefs are well placed, but there is a serious oversubscription of such participants, in which case it looks to others as a form of *malinvestment* driven by herding. This in reality is nothing but a transient in natural supply-versus-demand mechanics.

There was a cartoon in a 1972 issue of the *New Yorker*[32] showing a bench of Supreme Court justices, with the justice on the end saying, "Well, heck! If all you smart cookies agree, who am I to dissent?" This illustrates one of the most pernicious forms of group-think, stemming from deference to the opinion of others, even in light of one's own contrary conclusions. In his book *The Legal Analyst*,[33] Ward Farnsworth, a law professor, explores many legal aspects of information cascades. To mitigate this form of group-think, he discusses how in various military courts, officers vote in reverse rank order. By having the lowest-ranking officers vote first, they are prevented from the temptation to vote in sympathy with more senior officers.

There is a very small and simple rule set that mitigates a lot of groupthink problems. It may seem like an oversimplification to claim that there exits such a simple rule set, but consider the following: in order for large groups to synchronously do anything without requiring a centralized and orchestrating element, the rules for group behavior *have to be* simple. Otherwise, order would break down, chaos would ensue, and there would be no synchronized group dynamic. Thus, rules to mitigate problematic groupthink are symmetrically also simple. This is why information cascades, while powerful, are also said to be "fragile" and vulnerable to a quick demise. And why, thus far, anything with a whiff of fraud tends to get eaten alive in hours or days on crowd-funding sites.

James Surowiecki, author of *The Wisdom of Crowds* and presenter of "Independent Individuals and Wise Crowds, or Is It Possible to Be Too Connected?,"[34] asserts that when crowds are absent from proper decision-making environments, the decision makers can lose the benefits of collective wisdom, which can mean that their decisions will be narrowed down to the judgments of a few. To prevent this, Surowiecki presents a few mitigating recommendations:

1. *Diversity of opinion:* People should rely on their own interpretation of the facts.
2. *Independence:* Opinions should not be determined by the opinions of those around them.
3. *Decentralization:* People should draw on their own local knowledge.
4. *Aggregation:* People need a means to convert private judgments into a collective decision.

One area not addressed in these recommendations, and something essential to crowd dynamics in the connected world, is to empower affinity groups. The connected crowd isn't represented by a structureless graph, with random interconnectivities. Rather, microstructures arise, and for good reason. A combination of decentralization and specialization is what makes large organizations function well and yet allow tolerance for bad inputs, similar to the structure of our brain. Thus, we would be inclined to add the following:

5. *Affinity groups:* People need a means to identify, empower, and quickly assess the abilities of affinity groups, including their capacity to hold relevant local knowledge.

Valuations

Public valuations have been crowdsourced since mankind has traded goods, and certainly in capital markets. Except for some current-day aberrations (for example, high-frequency trading, extreme leverage, or derivatives), the price discovery of the "invisible hand" of the market has reigned. We're so used to being part of the supply-versus-demand pricing equation, whether buying goods at the store or equities on the stock exchanges, that we forget we're part of it. Ironically, except for in crowdfunding, when it comes to financing start-ups, we've traditionally thrown all of that out the window, and we've let a few parties with special interests set the prices. So it's always a source of amusement when people ask how a crowd of people would be any good at valuating start-ups. How can the market set a market price? Maybe a better question would be, "How can a very limited number of individual investors set the price?"

Fortunately, a number of modern efforts are proving that markets of people can indeed provide valid pricing for start-ups in the same way they provide pricing for nearly everything else. SharesPost,[35] SecondMarket,[36] and Private Equity Exchange[37] all either specialize on or include the trading of private company shares. A number of heavy-hitter investors are said to be loading up on their favorite private company stocks using these sites. Although it wasn't planned as such, there's an incidental by-product of these sites: they validate the ability for markets to adequately price private stocks for crowdfunding. If one were to combine the concept of a rolling close in funding with an open market price discovery mechanism, then crowdfunding promises to be a more natural market system that can handle projects from start to finish (or at least to the IPO).

Long Tails and Shrinking Heads

The *long tail* is jargon for a frequency distribution that essentially shows the popularity of items as plotted across all of the items. It's usually drawn as a *power-law graph*, showing the few ultrapopular items with high Y values on the left, and the curve ever asymptotically approaching the X axis as it progresses rightward, toward the least popular items. Why the long tail gets so much buzz is because while any one item on the right side (that is, the *tail*) of the curve has low popularity, the aggregate area of the tail is very considerable—simply put, there is a huge number of less popular items in the tail, and they add up significantly.

Online e-tailing is a classic example of that, showing that there is a healthy aggregate market for smaller volumes of niche goods, markets that conventional retailers have not well served, often because they are each individual markets that "won't move the needle." Crowdfunding is, in many ways, such a *long tail proposition*; there are so many early-stage projects that don't receive the attention of bigger investors, yet the aggregate amount of potential projects is unfathomably high.

But there are some important macroaspects of crowdfunding's future to consider, and these indicate a reshaping of the associated power-law curve to come. First, it's thought that existing funding mechanisms handle only a small percentage of funding demands—there's hardly a "head" to begin with. And as crowdfunding presents opportunities for the bigger money to join, in kind of a hybrid fashion, we'll have more of an integrative funding scenario. Extending the metaphor to the observations of Malone in *The Future of Work*, the body will stay large, but the head will decentralize (into the tail). When we're seeing high-quality films being produced for $10 million or $20 million instead of $200 million, the head has to shrink, or at least there will be a lot more films in the tail. Get ready for fatter tails and shrinking heads.

Gender Equalization

It's no secret that VC and angel investing are "clubby" activities, dominated mostly by middle-aged men. A quick survey of the partner biography pages at many popular VC firms reveals this stark gender inequity.

According to a 2007 study of angel investors in North America,[38] 86 percent were male with an average age of 57. Women didn't fare any better in a similar U.K. study,[39] where 93 percent of investors were male. Unfortunately, a similar trend also exists on the entrepreneur side: only 8 percent of companies that receive venture capital funding are run by women.

While the VC community seems stuck in an old boys' network mentality, crowdfunding is radically reshaping business investment and neutralizing gender bias, for both investors and entrepreneurs. Now, if there were a natural gender bias in both venture investing and venture creation, then Venture Capital would have a "leg to stand on." But according to Danae Ringelmann, cofounder of crowdfunding site Indiegogo, 42 percent of successful funding campaigns are led by women.[40] That's nearly *identical* to the 41 percent of small businesses in the United States that are run by women! It seems the "glass ceiling,"[41] which has been in place for millennia, is finally shattering.

PART II

THE CROWDFUNDING CAMPAIGN

Inheritance gives us spark. Community gives us fire.

—Anonymous

Chapter | 6

BENEFITS

What we gave, we have;
What we spent, we had;
What we left, we lost.
–Tryon Edwards[1]

In America alone, some 60 million people were considered among the "underbanked" in 2009, according to a Center for Financial Services Innovation (CFSI) study[2] based on Federal Deposit Insurance Corporation (FDIC) data. *Underbanked consumers* are those individuals who, while possibly having checking or savings accounts, also rely on alternative financial services such as money orders, check cashing, payday loans, and pawnshops. Even blindly applying the same metrics at the global scale would leave us to believe that well over 1 billion people in the world fall into this category.

But really, that is just a fraction of the population who have inadequate opportunity to access capital for their business ventures and personal projects. Let's call these people the *undercapitalized*.

And how many of these people want to create products, services, or entertainment that other people want? Are there no undercapitalized people who want to create locally grown food products that others in their community would enjoy consuming? Are there no undercapitalized innovators who want to create physical gadgets for smartphones? Are none of these people film artists who want to make documentaries about important contemporary topics? Of course, there are many people who fit these descriptions, and then some. And they collectively represent an enormous, untapped marketplace of economic activity at all levels of scale, from hyperlocal to hyperglobal.

It's easy to assign this disconnect in capital needs to barriers in the banking system. But at issue isn't so much the banking system. Rather, it is how or why we use the banking system. Banks are very capable of moving funds between the accounts of person A and person B, given that transferring funds is a very mechanical and passive process that scales well, including across national boundaries. But what on earth do banks know about validating the market for your endeavor or about hooking you up with like-spirited team members? Do they bring their fan base into your equation by retweeting your urgent messages? Is the bank president going to be in your play? Any chance the banks will fund your documentary about banking scandals? Lots of luck. These are just not activities that today's banks are set up to do. The banks operate based on purely passive and readily measurable metrics such as credit scores, incomes, expenses, and cash flows. These are conditions that put banks in the awkward position of being, as Bob Hope said, "a place that will lend you money if you can prove that you don't need it."[3]

At a high level, our current ills in capital formation come from that fact that we traditionally don't access capital from an open marketplace, or community if you will. Seeking financing from people (be they bankers or VCs) who are paid to mostly say no to risky deals doesn't constitute an open marketplace. And in the end, what you get if successful is mostly capital. The crowdfunding campaign is, by contrast, a way to access many types of resources from the marketplace. Capital certainly is one key resource, and what better way to obtain that than via market financing? But there are many other equally important resources that come from tapping into and becoming part of a community. What's more, every person who comes to the table with various elements of trust, passion, ideas, a network, a mission, or something else to offer, starts out from a position of worth to at least some group of other people. This is a breath of fresh air after decades of centralization by the financial world, which has stripped out many important elements of why people invest in each other, excepting for those that can be expressed by mathematical formulas such as price/earnings (P/E) ratios and profit margins. But it also means that the way we present our story, seeking the assistance of others, needs to be refactored. There is much more to be gained from the process, and each person has much more to offer. Maybe some old-school financial types won't like to hear this, but as a fund-raiser, you matter. Your story matters. Backers are along for the ride with you. Your banker gave you two colors to paint with: black and white. But with crowdfunding campaigns, we get to paint with vibrant colors.

Money

There is a direct correlation between the size of the initial community that crowdfund campaigners bring to the table and the amount that their project typically can raise.[4] While it's possible to overcome this with industriousness and/or a powerful story, it's not a problem in as much as it is an indicator that community financing works. Communities value the trust network that crowdfund campaigners bring, along with the entire body of buzz that others are willing to afford those people. If you can't kindle the fire with people you know, it's going to be really hard to convince people you don't know to throw logs on it. No matter how spontaneous or whimsical a campaign may seem, the reality is that the people behind it have built up to it their entire lives because their lives are part of the story. Whatever your story is, you're the action. And you're offering others a piece of that action.

To get access to money, you need to exchange value. Fortunately, a story, passion, vision, and a sense of mission all have value. Much of the art and science of obtaining money for your project center around your ability to craft your story, to build relationships that allow you to access the right audiences and to continuously promote your value proposition by way of offering the opportunity to be part of your story to other people. We shall talk about those activities soon. Hopefully it will become clear that the money raised is just a small fraction of the value exchange and opportunity from reaching out.

Marketing

One of the single most powerful aspects of an effective financial outreach using crowdfunding is that it develops a community of supporters—not an "audience," but a community. If marketing was relatively more passive and compartmentalized in classic business financing, it is now more interactive and dynamic. At hand is not only a fundamental shift in the field of marketing itself but actually an integration of marketing with many other parts of the economic paradigm. Where else would you find that many of the same cadre of people who fund you are also part of your marketing department? And that they buy your product or service?

Until the advent of crowdfunding, the relentless pursuit of selling an increasing amount of stuff that has had a decreasing level of quality and real value, has driven the field of marketing to degenerate into what might better be called a mass market manipulation scheme. That is the inevitable fate of a business model that is disconnected from a real value exchange and that does not build real communities. When the value exchange becomes asymmetrically in favor of the seller, managing the perception of the buyer often becomes an imperative.

The marketing world is all abuzz with its modern meme of "engaging customers." Now that's certainly a noble goal. Of course, engaging customers for the long term requires delivering a continuous exchange of real value and development of relationships with customers. That's kind of hard to do on any scale of time or number of people unless the customers are truly participating. What exactly is a relationship without participation? In the economics world, this act is typically referred to as *consumption*. But there's a seemingly unwavering hope that, after crafting a communication with the right messaging by marketing and getting it okayed by legal and potential partners, this latest expression of the company's core mission will develop huge customer engagement—as measured by the ratio of those who click the Like button.

Well, note to marketing departments everywhere: crowdfunding is the new Like button! Want to know if people are really interested in your new product? Why not find out? Anyone can push Like; people with at least some level of engagement push "Fund." Getting people to that point forces a discipline of true engagement. Real value has to be exchanged, be it physical or emotional. Without a doubt, "marketeers" will try to game this as well. But with crowdfunding being an open market and with so many projects offering forms of engagement that do offer real appeal to real people, those projects will live and die by their merits. The art and science of selling gives way to preselling, customer investment, participatory business, and other more credible forms of engagement.

Using many social networking tools, it's easy to send or forward messages out to contacts across other social media. This is of course no different with crowdfunding. Even for an ultralow $1 contribution to a rewards-based crowdfunding campaign, many of the platforms give contributors an immediate opportunity to send out "I funded project XYZ" notices. But there's a nontrivial difference. While sending out messages with links to articles you read says, "This is where I spent some time," sending out funding messages says, "This is where I spent some commitment."

As we shall soon discuss, ideally a crowdfunding campaign should turn contributors into marketers by continually engaging people in ways that keep adding value to their lives. When people have a sense of commitment and true engagement, they will often want to help. And even in the event that full funding goals are not reached, the community buzz process has been started, and it can lead to other, sometimes serendipitous, benefits.

Many business development and marketing aspects are being integrated and infused with crowdfunding, allowing for a more interactive and iterative process. For example, a smaller initial campaign can be launched to prove demand through presales. This "testing-the-waters" campaign helps mitigate risks associated with larger following campaigns, as it allows time to test and refine the marketing strategy. And it provides time to build relationships and obtain valuable feedback. In short, it's possible to more naturally scale into a dynamic market space with crowdfunding.

As an aside, as exciting and new as it seems to use crowdfunding to make the entire business process more dynamic and the role of customers more participatory, the concept of "mass customization" has been around for decades, the phrase coined in 1987 by Stan Davis in his book *Future Perfect*.[5] One type of such customization, termed "collaborative customization," was introduced in 1997 by James Gilmore and B. Joseph Pine in *The Four Faces of Mass Customization*.[6] To get to this level of customization, according to the thinking, the customer has to be involved in the product characteristics throughout the design process. But perhaps the most relevant intersection with crowdfunding was expressed in the 2004 paper from Frank Piller, Kathrin Moeslein, and Christof

Stotko entitled "Does Mass Customization Pay? An Economic Approach to Evaluate Customer Integration."[7] Their summary should have been entitled "The Benefits of Crowdfunding":

> We coin the term "economies of integration" to sum up these saving potentials. Economies of integration arise from three sources:
>
> 1. From postponing some activities until an order is placed
>
> 2. From more precise information about market demands
>
> 3. From the ability to increase loyalty by directly interacting with each customer

"Mass production" used to elicit imagery of giant warehouse-sized buildings populated with mechanized assembly lines. Today, it has taken on a whole new and more human meaning.

Participation and Emotional Attachment

There are scarcely any true one-way transactions. Even people who have the most giving of intents get the warm feeling of having helped someone in return. Every single bit that your story, product, mission, and/or actions returns back to people who fund you creates that much more of a two-way street. Assuming you believe that your project has any redeeming value, it's good to be fully conscious of the bidirectional flow of value from your project, starting from its inception. With that in mind, as a campaigner, it's much easier to frame the relationship between other people and you. If this seems obvious, then have a look at a number of rewards-based campaigns; many of them ask for "donations." Why use this extremely passive and one-directional term for people who are providing opportunity and are buying into the story? Perks aside, is there nothing else these campaigns offer in return?

Chances are when people provide money, they're really into what you're doing. You have started providing value to their lives already. If the thrust of the project is not financial or product based, then why not at least ask people to "contribute"? Or better yet, why not use a much more active and vibrant term such as "participate." Campaigns live or die by the amount of sharing that transpires before and during the campaign. The last thing you want to aim for is passive "donors." The good news is that if people are into what you're doing, many of them will want to help out in ways that you may not even have thought of yet. They may be able to connect your project with resources, such as a web programmer, studio time, or equipment. Maybe they know influencers who can name-drop your project in an important venue. Who knows? Maybe they work at a copy shop or graphics design shop and can hook you up with flyers. Or perhaps they can just generally help spread your story. In fact, everything that they can do to help makes them that much more part of, and invested in, your story. It's important to elicit, rather than to solicit. There is so much more to offer to the world than to just beg for money. Imagine some people who are having a relatively dull day. Their day may spring to life because of your project. Maybe you're offering something that people have been waiting for years to get involved with. Wherever possible, allow people to be active participants in your story.

Participation can start long before you pull the trigger on the campaign. Get your inner circle involved; they can review your campaign or help you get started building relationships you will need during the campaign. It can extend all the way through the campaign and into life thereafter. There's a really heartfelt example of the power of participation in a podcast interview with Chris Jones (author and filmmaker) and Danae Ringelmann (founder of Indiegogo).[8] Jones invited contributors to come and participate on the set or during any of the steps of making his film *Gone Fishing*.

He describes an experience in which he had one of the contributors sit below the camera during a take of a very emotional, intimate scene. When the lead actress started crying, he turned around to find the contributor having tears streaming down her face. She had no idea how emotional and intimate the filmmaking process could be, and she left with an enormous impression. For a £50 contribution, she got more than she imagined from the experience.

Understanding the dynamics of crowdfunding participation comes largely from answering the question of *why*. One of the more powerful observations about why certain social leaders and businesses alike tend to be far more successful comes from Simon Sinek, who gave a related TED talk.[9] He calls this observation the "golden circle theory of marketing." In this theory, there are simply three concentric circles, labeled "why," "how," and "what" from inner to outer, respectively. This, he claims, corresponds to the way the brain is organized. Most people and companies try to connect through the "what" outer circle, by offering details and facts. This is often a less successful path to connecting with people because the corresponding "what" part of the brain houses our logic. Thus it's hard to get anyone truly excited or motivated or to form a deep connection by starting here and working inward.

Highly successful leaders operate completely in the opposite order, as exemplified by Dr. Martin Luther King. The rationale is that people don't buy *what* you do. They buy *why* you do it. Dr. King was famous for his "I Believe" and "I Have a Dream" speeches. He didn't parade around with an "I Have a 20-Point Plan" speech, as a number of politicians often do. When he talked about his beliefs, he attracted people who believed what he believed. And some of those people made his cause their own, and they helped get the word out to more people who believed. And his belief really spoke to the *why*: "Not until all of the laws which are made by man are consistent with the laws that are made by a higher authority, will we live in a just world." As a result, 250,000 people showed up to hear him speak, 25 percent of whom were white. As Sinek says, "If you hire people just because they can do a job, they'll work for your money. But if you hire people who believe what you believe, they'll work for you with blood and sweat and tears."

For another fine example of why, have a look at James Victore's web page.[10] In bold letters, his mission statement reads: "We want to work with people and companies who believe that the status quo is not enough, that good work matters, and that design can be a tool to affect opinions and culture." He's hosting an event, Take This Job & Love It, described as, "A one-day live event about work, life, and bucking the status quo. Come reclaim your creativity, ignite your path to personal greatness, and access a higher level of badass-dom." That's *why*. And if you dig around, you'll find out who he is: an author, self-taught, independent award-winning artist, designer, and animator, and design professor at the School of Visual Arts in New York. That's an impressive background in its own right, but first he starts with *why*.

Deep and intertwined in humanity is a fundamental need to connect on the level of who we are and why we do what we do. That should never be overlooked in terms of the value that participation in each other's projects offers to all parties. And given the ever-increasing popularity of crowdfunding, it foretells a more social and values-based approach in the way that individuals and businesses connect and interact with each other. Tell them *why*.

Currying Serendipity

Something quite amazing happens whenever people open themselves to a greater audience. Other people seem to "come out of the woodwork." They can be people with similar interests, people who just find the project exciting or interesting, people who have various resources that you need, or people looking to join your team. Maybe they're downstream investors who want to keep an eye on how your project develops, or they're professional service providers. In any case, you never really know where your campaign will lead you, but it's likely to be a lot more exciting ride than you bargained for. And it will probably be a lot different from what you had anticipated. This is a phenomenon that occurs across so many fields that have public exposure, including blogging, open source, and crowdfunding. While at times it's reasonable to assume that at least some people will be interested in what you have to offer, it's hard to know exactly whom those people will end up being. This is part of the magic of reaching out to the community instead of remaining confined to narrow and existing channels.

Morrie Warshawski, author of *Shaking the Money Tree*, coined the phrase "currying serendipity." He encourages his clients "to actively engage in activities that have a high likelihood of encouraging positive and unexpected opportunities to come their way."[11] That's a recipe to make many parts of our lives more exciting. Wouldn't it be great if our education system were also built around the concept?

In the opening of *The Monk and the Riddle: The Art of Creating a Life While Making a Living*,[12] Randy Komisar tells the story of a monk who hopped a long ride with him on his motorcycle, only to seek to return home after reaching the destination. What was the point of all this? Well, he wanted to go for the ride. Even if currying serendipity isn't your main goal, keep in mind that it is for many people out there who may want to be part of your ride. And they may just take up your cause.

Returns, Rewards, and Perks

In the pre-Kickstarter era, philanthropy and investing were far more socially discrete activities, seemingly living in different regions in our collective consciousness. How things have changed! Crowdfunding has opened up opportunities to reach out and access many forms of value, and it has offered at least as many in return. Even before the recent regulatory change in the United States allowing for securities-based crowdfunding, which of course previously forced platforms to have a bias in the styles of rewards that campaigners could offer, there was and continues to be a lot of creativity in casting rewards that hue toward the financial and business sides of things while trying to avoid regulatory issues. As various countries and regions unlock the economic and social power of crowdfunding, and as businesses discover until-now-missed opportunities, the forms of rewards offered in crowdfunding will continue broadening and become more integrated. Certainly, biases will remain, if not flourish, as some platforms customize and adapt for specific markets. But the major trend is integration, driven by the power of market demand from all parties involved.

Speaking of change, Jason Calacanis, an angel investor and founder of the popular start-up conference and competition LAUNCH,[13] posted an article in February 2012 entitled "The Two Most Important Startups in the World."[14] And his picks: AngelList and Kickstarter! These two start-ups are veritable crowdfunding "bookends," living at what used to be opposite ends of the crowdfunding bookshelf: AngelList, as its name implies, is angel investor centric, and Kickstarter hails from the rewards camp. Calacanis continued in his characteristic attention-grabbing headline style: "They're more important than Facebook, Twitter, and Apple. Heck, they're more important than Pinterest! (← zing! pow!)." It doesn't take much to imagine that with the recent regulatory change, AngelList will expand into and engage the more open and broad general investor frontier, and the many rewards style of crowdfunding platforms will expand to include angel networks. But rather than a head-on collision in the middle, the intersection of platforms will be more a story of integrating the pieces that make sense to the niches they serve. As a result, some platforms will directly compete, others not so much. In any case, the dynamic of opening up to a wider spectrum is a good thing because it means far more value can be exchanged in all directions.

Beyond that, more open and integrated systems bode well for a return to quality, a trend that was identified by the *Trends Journal's Top 12 Trends 2012* report: "In the bleak terrain of 2012 and beyond, 'Affordable Sophistication' will direct and inspire products, fashion, music, the fine arts, and entertainment at all levels. U.S. businesses would be wise to wake up and tap into the dormant desire for old time quality and the America that was."[15] One has only to look to the nonprofit space to see the dichotomy in quality resulting from tightly controlled and often unfairly advantaged corporate behavior. In fact, a main finding in an interesting paper, "Crowdfunding of Small Entrepreneurial Ventures,"[16] was that nonprofit organizations tend to be more successful in achieving their fund-raising targets. The paper suggests "that a possible explanation for this result stems from the fact that not-for-profit organizations may be more prone to commit to high-quality products or services if quality comes at the expense of quantity." Essentially, this boils down to choice. An open, uncontrolled system offers choice. A return to choice is a return to quality. And along with that comes an enormous potential for reengagement in the products people buy, the entertainment they enjoy, the food they eat, and the communities they interact with. Even for the most hard-core capitalists among us, this trend cannot be ignored.

In 1995, Clayton Christensen shattered the then-current business conscious when he introduced a new concept in his article "Disruptive Technologies: Catching the Wave" in the *Harvard Business Review*.[17] The concept of disruptive technologies was further explored in his popular books on innovation, and it is now part of a respectable business education. In a nutshell, the idea is that big companies tend to focus on their current "cash cow" or mainline customers and miss the boat on the next wave of innovation. The eternal pioneer in business thinking, Christensen has been more recently advocating for a change in focus of business metrics. Rather than the cost-oriented "bean counter" metrics such as return on net assets, he instead favors the Net Promoter Score (NPS), which is the measuring of customer loyalty by way of simply asking customers how likely they are to recommend the company to a friend. Why? Because, as Steve Denning, contributor at *Forbes*, writes: "As a result of epochal shift of power in the marketplace from seller to buyer, the *customer* is now in charge. We now live in the age of customer capitalism. Making money and corporate survival now depend not merely on pushing products at customers but rather on delighting them so that they *want* to keep on buying."[18]

Alone, a shift of the corporate mindset toward customer-centric metrics will be painful and it will likely take a long time. But even then it will end up, at least partly, at the wrong destination because the entire perspective of the corporation-customer relationship is flawed from the outset. We need to reach mental escape velocity from the archaic producer-consumer business paradigm, catapulting us back into the last few centuries. Whether a big or small enterprise, a nonprofit organization, or an individual, we are all participants in a multidirectional network of opportunity. Leadership *produces* opportunity for participation. Followers then *consume* opportunity by participating. What's salient is that all parties actively participate, at least on some level, by exchanging value.

Many of the more active participants will then add their own inspiration or perspiration, and they will produce further value that will be beneficial to other parties including the initial leadership. Which raises the question, who is the producer and who is the consumer? The risk of using an NPS-like metric is that it stops at an assessment of "customer loyalty." In social networking terms, that's akin to measuring how many people push the Like button. Well, what about measuring how active and engaged customers are? Perhaps we'll call this the Active Customer Engagement (ACE) metric. What percent of customers are actively submitting ideas for new or enhanced products? Did any of them translate your product announcements into their own language? How many new purchases came from existing customers? Did they open the doors to local manufacturers? "Like" was the measurement of yesteryear; today it's "Love." As hockey superstar Wayne Gretzsky would advise, skate to where the puck will be.

It's given that the focus of some cross-section of contributors will have a more narrow financial and transactional focus. But in the big picture, value comes from framing the returns and rewards such that they evoke massive participation. As says the Kickstarter blog on interesting campaigns related to current news, "The backers and creators of these projects didn't just respond to the news of the day. They helped create it."[19] As the body of thought that gave us the notion of gross domestic product (GDP) as a measurement of economic health fades in relevancy, replacing it are measures of real value to people. Perhaps the P in GDP should instead stand for *participation* or *purpose*. Perhaps this is already reflected in the fact that the United Nations International Year of Cooperatives was celebrated in 2012,[20] a substantial indicator of the changing tide and the trend toward cooperation.

A better and more holistic way to assess returns is in the eyes of the individuals or organizations who receive them in a value exchange for whatever they offered up. There's no reason to belabor the situation for those seeking purely financial returns. But examples of crowdfunding with nontraditional returns are legion. One would be Atlantis Books, a tiny bookstore occupying the basement of a cliff-top villa on the island of Santorini, Greece, and overlooking the Aegean. More than a bookstore, Atlantis has been host to many cultural events such as bookmaking, dinners, literature readings, film and other festivals, and even weddings. But after seven years of operation, the Greek economic collapse and subsequent plummeting in tourism rates took a bite out of the company's book sales. The owners were forced to slim down and change their business model, which had included launching their own in-house publishing outfit: Paravion Press.

To reinvigorate Atlantis with its new model and to purchase new book stock needed to regain profitability in the "post-crash Kindle-powered years," Atlantis reached out to like-minded people in its crowdfunding campaign,[21] subtitled "A Small Bookstore with a Big Ask." Actually, their $40,000 ask, which they successfully raised, wasn't really that sizable by crowdfunding standards. After some quality time in awe of the stunning view of the Aegean and the village in the video and website pictures, have a look at their $130-level contribution reward: "Next time you're in Greece, you've got a bookstore with a bed with your name on it because you're keeping Atlantis Books alive. And we'll paint you up on that spiral, loud and proud." Now for anyone with a love of literature, that would be a very reasonably priced stay and a lasting experience. Lasting enough that your name would have been added to the spiral written on the ceiling of the names of people who have stayed in and supported the bookshop.

Chapter | 7

THE ARTFUL ASK

It's not the load that breaks you down;
it's the way you carry it.
—Lena Horne[1]

B ased on decades of experience from his groundbreaking work with the severely addicted, Dr. Gabor Maté's newest book, *In the Realm of Hungry Ghosts*,[2] shatters the status quo notion that many ailments of the human condition can be attributed to isolated factors, such as genetics. He argues that it's not possible to separate the health of individuals from the social and political system in which they live. Many problems such as heart disease, high blood pressure, miscarriages, and a whole range of other health problems can be shown to have little correlation with genetics. In reality, they are strongly correlated with stressful and isolating environments.

In a recent address, "Capitalism and Addiction,"[3] Dr. Maté reveals some intriguing observations. According to an Australian study involving breast tissue biopsies, neither emotional stress nor emotional isolation were correlated with the chances that the biopsies were cancerous when only one of these factors applied to a given patient. Yet, based on psychological interviews of the women before their biopsy results were known, a combination of emotional stress *and* isolation led to a probability nine times greater (relative to the average) that the results were cancerous! While being alone with stress manifests in some very negative ways, as Maté explains, even small sharing experiences can instantaneously and positively transform the physiology of a person who is otherwise isolated. A smile may change someone's day, but sharing can change his or her life.

We, as a people, have a strong physiological and psychosocial need to be connected. Sharing our stresses and our excitement is how we are wired to exist as social beings. These are acts that deliver important value to our lives. And thus, any form of economics that is compatible with the human condition must necessarily and naturally integrate into our social fabric. Unfortunately, decades of onerous regulation and centuries of financial centralization have devastatingly unraveled our social fabric's ability to integrate capital formation, leaving us hanging by a few threads connected to large institutions. Is it surprising that investing in public securities of large transnational corporations that we are out of touch with provides little social benefit? Or, do you throw neighborhood block parties every quarter when Apple files its 10-Q?[4]

The expression "hungry ghosts" is quite symbolic of the insatiable emptiness that stems from our investment landscape, which has been mostly strip-mined of its social vibrance and value. We are hungry to connect. Sometimes we seek help. Sometimes we want to provide it. And sometimes we just want to be part of other people's stories. But at a high level, we are all driven to participate in *natural human economics*, which we might loosely define as the participation in the creation and exchange of value among people. In this light, it becomes a lot more apparent what makes crowdfunding tick, including why people want to participate so strongly in other people's dreams.

We will reach a greater appreciation for crowdfunding, and for social networking at large, when these activities cease to be an escape from our daily lives, but rather become culturally and economically part of our lives. With this mindset, it's far more intuitive to understand and run an effective crowdfunding campaign. Whether it be rewards- or return on investment–based crowdfunding, we are all in it for benefit. We are exchanging value and transacting natural human economics. Purely mathematical transactions are out. Developing relationships through which we can exchange value is in. And of consequence, through these relationships there is a potential for massive benefit to our collective health.

Authenticity: Keeping It Real

After being inundated in a sea of corporate marketing and branding efforts, it's at times easy to lose sight of the value of our own personal brand. Yes, that's right, we are our own brand. And when people reach out to the community for any form of participation, their brand matters. That's *brand* not in the sense of hyped-up presence, spin, and other hyperbolic nonsense that borders on propaganda but *brand* that speaks to the core of personal trust, motives, mission, passion, and a value proposition. Unfortunately, much of our big-corporation branding is predicated on their ability to overwhelm the market with their messaging in every conceivable venue, effectively underwhelming consumers' ability to access other choices. For example, one of Coca-Cola's most famous slogans is "Coke is it." In reality, there's pretty much just Coke and Pepsi. If you prefer one of the other brands, chances are it's owned by Coke or Pepsi. What in that slogan says anything about the value that the company offers in its products or as a corporation? Nothing. It doesn't need to because Coke *is* it.

But for the rest of us, interest from others is a function of who we are and what we have to offer. Being real beats being really slick. Without the asymmetric advantage of the corporate marketing machine, authenticity reigns, or shall we say, returns to its reign. So rather than spin, showcase yourself and team, your passion, and certainly your story. People who contribute are buying a ticket to be part of your story. Ironically, many people who consider using crowdfunding initially don't want to be in their pitch video. But that's almost always counterproductive. *Of course* people want to know who you are, imperfections and all. A consistent message from a collective of successful campaigners is to let people see your eyes, let them see your passion. That's a huge part of your brand. Tell them your story. By all means, include your previous successes and relationships with others in the community, as well as other forms of "social proof." These are all part of your story.

And if it's truly the case, tell them about the extraordinary circumstances in your own lives that gave you no choice but to do this project! This was a salient point made by Joke Fincioen and Biagio Messina (affectionately known as Joke & Biagio), who crowdfunded[5] *Dying to do Letterman*.[6] They decided to make this award-winning indie documentary, about their friend and comedian Steve Mazon's dream to do stand-up comedy on the Letterman show, after finding out about his terminal case of cancer. Now, not everybody's story includes putting his or her own personal finances on the line to help another person live a dream, but we can all take away a message about the power of being human from Mazon's motto: "Live your dream, or die trying." And it speaks to the heart of what any type of investor needs to see, which is "skin in the game." It's hard to convince other people to participate unless you reek of commitment. And this is one of the few scents that manages to pass through the Internet.

Of course, standing in the way of really getting the story out are all the "fears from our peers" that we have, such as the fears of failure and rejection. And certainly from laying all our cards on the table, especially when we don't have the best hand of cards.

Perhaps the most potent of fears is that of failure. So many would-be entrepreneurs never take the next step because of the "what would people think of me if I fail" factor. There was an interesting and relevant blog post from James Victore, iconoclastic designer, design professor, and author of "Victore or, Who Died and Made You Boss?"[7] about shyness. As a design professor, he does an impromptu survey of his class, simply asking who in the group believes they are shy. And the result he states is that "inevitably, at least three-quarters of the students raise their hands, . . . albeit only shoulder high."[8] What's really telling is in his observation about the root of shyness:

> Most of us are so afraid of failing that we don't even risk it. And what's worse, risk and rejection become something to avoid at all costs. A habit is formed. We close doors that may lead to opportunities and stop putting ourselves out there for other people to respond to. This fear of rejection is normal. Everyone shies away and has moments, or extended moments, of self-doubt. But the fear is also a test. It means you are onto something and you should pay attention to it and not shy away.

Often, our worst critics are our inner ones, combined with a few outer ones in our close friends and family circle. Those mechanisms were important to help "protect us" at a time when those same critics were mostly the only and core support group. But now we can reach out to find many other people with similar interests, and thus "fitting in" has less relevance or, shall we say, less locality. And thus today, the act of putting yourself out there is more a personal decision of whether you seek critics or comrades. It's quite obvious from a survey of crowdfunding campaigns that those who focus on finding comrades are far more successful.

Fundamentally people want to participate because they want to invest in a ticket to your journey, financial or otherwise. So don't mask the journey, and don't hide behind the curtain. If formulaic was truly what people desired, there would be no time for crowdfunding because we would all be consumed watching hundreds of channels of formulaic crap on TV. But instead, the indie film industry is exploding. As is indie music, food, news, local investing, and so on. Personalize and create desire for your success. Given that people are along for the ride, they receive the benefit of being part of your story. And speaking of stories, one of the most valuable lessons from being an entrepreneur is this: elevator pitches require push, but stories have natural pull. We are deeply wired to convey stories as part of our social makeup. Fortunately, we all have stories. If yours can capture enough attention and imagination and is based on a real desire, it has a lot of potential.

Impact and Appeal

Founder of Blacklight Films Louie Schwartzberg has spent decades filming time-lapse photography of flowers.[9] As you can see in his TED talk, whether it be in photography or cinematography, he has an extraordinary gift for creating work that elicits profound and visceral reaction. When people see his animated imagery of a flower coming to life, they'll often say, "Oh my God!" In his talk, he asks the question, "Have you ever wondered what that meant?" His explanation, as poetic as is his visual work, is something that elegantly conveys the essence of a true connection of his work to its beholders:

> The "oh" means it caught your attention, makes you present, makes you mindful. The "my" means it connects to something deep inside your soul. It creates a gateway for your inner voice to rise up and be heard. And "God," God is that personal journey we all want to be on, to be inspired, to feel like we're connected to a universe that celebrates life.

Of course, it may seem hard to foster this kind of deep connection for all kinds of projects that might be crowdfunded. But the idea is that for some number of people somewhere—be it by awe, by laughter, by the desire for an ultimate product, or by the money lust that investors get when they have a line on the next Facebook start-up—participating in your project offers at least a mini "religious moment." That's the impact to aim for, but first, there are some basic factors that can help the overall appeal.

According to a post from Yancey Strickler, cofounder of Kickstarter, "Projects with videos have had a success rate of 54 percent while ones without have had a success rate of 39 percent."[10] However, in the *2011–2012 Report on 150 RPG Crowdfunding Projects*, which is an analysis of gaming-specific crowdfunding campaigns, projects achieved successful funding 76 percent of the time with videos and 66 percent of the time without.[11] While this does statistically argue in favor of offering a teaser video, or *pitch clip* as it's affectionately called, the data by no means suggests that offering a video is a hard-and-fast rule. A lot of people espouse various top-10 lists of "must-dos" for the crowdfunding campaign, and the pitch clip is nearly always on the lists. To be fair, the campaigns that do include video tend to also raise more money, 122 percent more than those with text alone, according to Slava Rubin, cofounder of Indiegogo.[12] But as is the case for utilizing advice from others' experience in any other domain, it's best to load up the tool belt with each gem of wisdom, and then apply them judiciously as you see fit.

Without a doubt, we are very sensory creatures, and the visual element is a huge part of that, but we need to think about the approach in the context of the people who help spread our story. As elucidated in a post from prolific author Seth Godin (including *All Marketers Are Liars: The Power of Telling Authentic Stories in a Low-Trust World* and *Tribes: We Need You to Lead Us*): "A key element in the spread of ideas is their visual element. iPods and visual styles spread faster in the real world than ephemeral concepts. Pictures and short jokes spread faster online because the investment necessary to figure out if they're worth spreading is so tiny."

Let's instead look at the big picture and ask something for which the answer will give a better framework for determining how to shape the presence of the campaign. Namely, what is the most effective way to (1) immediately attract potentially interested people's attention to the project, (2) quickly form a connection between those people and your cause, and (3) answer the most pressing questions about the project that they would reasonably have?

The first glance that a potential contributor has, whether it be by random discovery on a portal or via a mention in an industry-appropriate venue, is likely to be an image—or at least, a body of text surrounding an image. Perhaps it's just a thumbnail image used in widgets placed on friends' websites. Whatever the size and fidelity are, the image needs to quickly attract the eyes of the intended audience. If each person gives you only a fraction of a second, what image would you use? Considering how much information any one person has access to, you have just a tiny window of time to set the initial hook. Have other people, preferably from the target audience, review this imagery if possible because it's other people that need to be attracted to it.

For those people who overcome the split-second eyeball time barrier, thanks to your amazing imagery, you have a matter of seconds to convey the basis of your campaign to them. If you can't convince them that they should invest a few minutes to dig deeper, get excited about all that you have to offer, and learn about your amazing story, then you'll probably lose them. Let them know straightaway what your campaign is about. If you have an incredibly powerful video, the question is, why would they decide to even watch it? In comedy, the punch line is at the end of the joke. But then again, the audience has already *committed* to buying a ticket and grabbing a seat, and they probably know the comedian's work already. Until you have some form of commitment from other people, the punch line usually goes at the beginning. Otherwise, people tend to quickly get that feeling of impatience and perceive the experience as a waste of their time.

Giving your story gravity starts with an enticing project name. Given the choice, why not pick one that resonates with people? As always, shop it around and get feedback from other people. If you can supply your own image headings that look good and stand out, that's a pretty powerful and simple improvement. As an example of beautiful and artistic headings, perhaps check out the campaign page for *Amanda Palmer: The new RECORD, ART BOOK, and TOUR*.[13] Besides the artistic touch, this project is a wonderful example of how it can pay to do it your own way. After finishing recording a new album, Amanda and her band needed money to promote, mix, and distribute their music and art book worldwide. But rather than given the more typical vocal pitch, she put a few words on each of a series of flash cards, and she held them up while playing a soundtrack from her band. Her music and imagery might not be for everyone, but apparently it's for a lot of people—with a funding goal of $100,000, she raised over $1 million! Chalk one up for being real.

Then there's the section for adding a textual description. In this section, keep it brief and to the point, especially in a summary section, which people first see. Until there is commitment to look at your project more deeply, people have an aversion to reading any more text than necessary. Provide images that truly define what you and your product are about. People are interesting to other people, and it's important to connect on a human level, so put yourself and your work in the pictures. And use imagery that elicits an immediate intrigue and interest level, tying in the emotional reasons that allow people to relate and connect. To the extent that this part of your story can include social proof and elements of your past work or experience, do consider adding it. The whole idea is to present the most engaging story as possible, in a very short amount of time, with the hope that people think something like, "Hey, *this* is interesting. I want to find out more." There are a lot of other things people could be doing and a lot of people pitching other projects. Your pitch has to have something special going on. Above all, keep it real and keep it interesting.

If you succeed in providing a "curb appeal" that convinces people that it's worth having a further look, then they may watch your video or have a look further at your materials. It's not necessarily the case that the primary page would include video. For example, really classy artwork from an artist who already possesses cachet may speak for itself. In that case, probably the focus would be on some really top-shelf images. In any case, even if video isn't of primary focus, video clips and links can be stored in a secondary page for people who want a deeper dive into the project and the team. Video is a great way to make the human connection, especially when the intended contributors are not already familiar with the campaigners and their past work.

If you offer video, then by all means try to be in it. Whatever you're doing, the fact that it has interested other people means that you're interesting to them. If you want to offer a longer video, then it's a good idea to have a teaser clip on the landing page, and then people can explore more if they like what they saw. And by the way, if you link to other clips or materials, it's best to link to materials stored on other parts of your project page—so you don't make it easy for people to get distracted on other sites and forget about you!

Be a real person in the video, tell people quickly and powerfully why your project has meaning, your story, and why they should be involved. In fact, if you have a team, put them all in the video—they're part of the story, and they make it that much more interesting. If there's an urgency involved, that's always a good thing to let shine through right from the beginning. People tend to like a sense of mission. And unless you're working the "fund me, I'm a catastrophe" play, speak from a position of strength. The idea is that you're offering value to other people. So don't beg or be apologetic. Rather, invite people to be part of your world-changing story.

Great lighting for pictures and video is something that has high impact yet is relatively easy and inexpensive to achieve. A number of video-bloggers have created their own somewhat professional looking studios in their garage using bed sheets and the proper lighting. Seriously, if you're not familiar with lighting techniques, have a quick read about "three-point lighting."[14] If you can't borrow the extra lights from someone you know, a trip to the hardware store will get the job done. Speak to someone you know who does photography—he or she will probably give you an earful. The quality of the shoot comes mostly from the lights, not the camera. And there's nothing better to light up than your face. Let people see your face and your eyes. If eyes are the windows to the soul, then they provide an amazing conduit for connecting to others via the pictures or video you provide. But as ears also play a role, so it's worth considering adding an awesome background soundtrack.

The culmination of your pitch should be a crystal clear "call to action." It may seem obvious to you, but what do you want people to do next? As the goal is probably to have them contribute, is the contribution facility easy to access and obvious? To people unfamiliar with crowdfunding, the process may be less than obvious to them. There's a fantastic way to shake out these issues and tune your pitch at the same time. Dry-run as much as possible of your pitch with people you know, including those who don't know much about your story or about using crowdfunding. Let them see it as a newly exposed person would. Find out how much of your pitch they understood after 10 seconds, and after a minute. What did they miss or not understand? What was the confusion? What mattered to them most? With a few iterations, you can quickly tune the pitch to be much more effective. The problem with pitching is that you already know your story, so you probably don't make its best critic.

Many entrepreneurs in the start-up world claim they didn't nail their pitch until about the third or fourth time. A similar trend is seen in performing well in job interviews. It's a good idea to get feedback and iterate quickly in your campaign as well.

The Team

The size of the campaign story matters, and at times that correlates to the team size. Teams on Indiegogo raise 70 percent more on average than campaigns run by just one person, according to founder Slava Rubin.[15] Of course, for the mathematically inclined, that does translate to 15 percent less money allocated for each person of a two-person team (and even worse percentage-wise for larger teams). But to be fair, funds for creative projects tend to be focused more on joint-effort costs, for example, production costs, than on income. If you ask angels and VCs what makes them really excited about otherwise risky and unproven start-ups, they respond almost universally with "the team" or "the founders." An investor that responds "the founder," in singular form, is a rarest of breed, up there with unicorns and leprechauns. Many investors will state outright that they "don't do solo entrepreneurs."

But let's have a look at the data and see what the investor checkbook says. CB Insights did a demographic study of first-round VC for Internet start-ups in the United States for the year 2010, entitled *Venture Capital Human Capital Report*.[16] This is a relatively unique study because it assembled a range of demographic information about early start-ups, such as gender, age, and race. And fortuitously, the number of founders. In California, two-person teams were the norm, at 51 percent, while one- and three-person teams made up 20 and 24 percent, respectively. But in Massachusetts, things were far different, with single founders making up 56 percent; two- and three-founder teams came in at 13 and 25 percent, respectively. Even more intriguing in the case of Massachusetts was the factoid that single founders raised more on average than two-founder teams! As soon as you make a "rule of thumb," your finger will get cut off.

This data certainly doesn't suggest basing the size of the team on anyone's data. But what nobody disputes is that the story does make a difference. It's typical in the start-up world to hear entrepreneurs saying, "We have to tighten up our story" (that is, the last investors they pitched *poked* holes in it) or "We need a better story" (that is, the last investors they pitched *blasted* holes in it). It's all about the story, and the team is a very important part of the story. Certainly, a group of people have the inherent potential to put forth a larger story. They also bring to the campaign a wider aggregated social network, experience, and perhaps even a base of admirers of their respective bodies of work. But those same values can also be brought by friends and contacts to the campaign of a single party. And of course, in some stories, the center of attraction is just one person.

To the extent that the team members have a material meaning to the story, by all means, they should be visually part of the campaign. Put them in the video and pictures. We all like to see the faces behind the story. Social proof and credibility of the team are important; those are often the starting points on the path toward establishing trust. Many campaigners, in all the excitement to get their campaigns launched, forget to weave into their stories personal backgrounds, experiences, and other factors relevant to building trust and credibility. Earlier success stories and experience can boost credibility, and certainly providing a variety of links to potential funders reduces the friction in the process.

Clear Goals

It's human nature to be forgiving of certain oversights. Forgetting to explain what you want to do with the funds sought doesn't make the list. It doesn't matter if the project is very philanthropic or capitalistic in nature—people want to know what comes of their money. That's part of the value exchange. Investors want the information because it's the beginning of their understanding and creation of the investment thesis. Even social contributors want to feel that their money has importance. Somewhere in the story, "the spend" has to appear. The more leanings a campaign has toward an investment, especially larger and later-stage ones, the more the information provided will need to look like a budget or other form of financial projection. For a campaign to fund an indie documentary about killer sea sponges, "We need money to rent a boat and scuba equipment" might be good enough. But man, put it in the pitch! So few rules work often enough, but this one is a no-brainer. Otherwise, the natural sentiment of potential contributors is that they're just throwing money into a black hole.

In fact, in the initial materials that contributors are exposed to, be they videos, pictures, or the textual descriptions, there are just a few must-haves that should be present—the rest really are situational. Without regard to the style of returns, these are unsurprisingly the same for any kind of campaign. Namely, tell people what the problem is, who are involved, why they are involved, where the action is, how the problem will be solved, and the timetable involved. This is, of course, basic structural information that people need to grasp the story. It's wisdom of timeless origin, but memorialized by Rudyard Kipling in his *Just So Stories* (1902), in which the verse of a poem reads:

I keep six honest serving-men
(They taught me all I knew);
Their names are What and Why and When
And How and Where and Who.[17]

Gathering the "five Ws," as they're called, is a principle behind investigative journalism and other forms of research. Each W solicits fundamental information that, when combined with the rest of the information, tends to form a more complete story. Whether we consciously acknowledge it or not, when we encounter a new story, our minds perform these interrogatives. So to make an effective pitch, put yourself in other people's shoes (well, actually their minds). Inquiring minds want to know. Pitch them clearly what they want to know.

Starting Fires with Influencers and Core Fans

While creating a lot of traction for crowdfunding campaigns may be a bit of an art, there is a lot of well-known science behind it. It involves many of the same strategies of making anything go viral. To analogize, you and your team want to start as many fires burning as possible. There are a limited number of team members, and there's a limited amount of time to make this happen. It's wildly more effective if you start your fires burning in areas that have plenty of dry kindling wood and that naturally carry the fire to much larger areas. By contrast, if you haphazardly run around with your torches, trying to light the rain-soaked undergrowth, you'll get nowhere quickly.

While you may get lucky with a scattershot approach, spamming so many uninterested people will leave a wake of irritation at best, and it may turn off someone you need further down the road who can swing a lot of influence. For sure, your cadre of core fans, family, and friends can provide the first-level support network for the campaign. Without them, you would have a lot less social proof to get the fires burning. But for a moment, it's important to step out of yourself and your immediate lives and think critically about who your supporters would be in the world. What blogs would they read, what forums would they engage in, and what radio shows would they listen to? Would they be part of specific organizations, or would they go to particular events?

Once you've made a conscious effort to identify these venues, then you should think about who the major influencers and gatekeepers are for each venue. *They* are the people who can really light your fire! A single post or mention from one of these people can easily be worth more than thousands of spam messages—not just in scale but in the fact that they can help you connect with truly engaged and interested supporters. And in the process, those major influencers may lend a bit of their credibility to your efforts. While the fire starts with your *close ties*, as they've been called, a crowdfunding campaign is a process of starting with your close ties and branching out to and discovering your *natural ties*—those supporters who would naturally want to have some form of connection but have not yet been introduced. But to get to enough natural ties, you may well have to go through influencers.

More and more often, people of major influence have achieved those positions from respect and accomplishment, at least where transparency and open market principles are involved. These *supernodes*, as they are sometimes called in social networking terms, are people that you'd really like to have pass your message along, simply because they are the hub of the hub-and-spoke pattern that connects to a lot of potentially interested supporters for your campaign (or other hubs). Supernodes are potential *relationship routers*. And that's exactly what thousands of other people are thinking.

Think about the endless torrent of requests they must get each day, to the tune of "Hey, can you promote XYZ for me?" from people they don't even know. It's critical to avoid this horrendous violation of social etiquette. What has proven much more effective is to approach people by opening up brief but genuine dialogues with them. It's not a bad idea to let them know that you've done at least some research into who they are. In the start-up world, there's an old adage that if you ask for money, you'll get an opinion, but if you ask for an opinion, you'll get money. "I've read your posts about XYZ. I'm making a film about XYZ. What do you think about this short clip?" is infinitely better than coming in with your guns blazing, demanding a retweet of a post with your campaign website address.

Relationships are developed. There's nothing magic about the Internet that changes this. If over time, you can develop relationships with influencers, they are far more likely to help spread the word when you are ready. And they just may be excited enough to participate further. If you're not set in stone on a particular direction, you may also get an opinion on what would make for an interesting project direction.

Campaigns often exhibit roughly three different phases, each one potentially requiring a different finesse to stoke the fire properly.[18] In the first phase, funding mostly comes from the close ties—friends, family, and fans. Often in successful campaigns, this phase will pick up a certain amount of momentum and excitement. But in the second phase, funding growth often slows as the more immediate network gets tapped out and the campaign transitions to second- and third-order networks—the networks of people who were reached by way of the first phase of the campaign. At this time, recommendations and all of the relationship building that the campaigners have done are essential to accessing these more distant networks. Getting a mention in an important venue can potentially supercharge this phase. And then when funding success becomes relatively obvious, the third ("race to be in") stage may well kick in. When there's a lot of excitement around what looks to be a successful funding, a number of lurkers or last-minute contributors may jump in and send the project to its funding goal in a quick burst.

Knowing about these phases as well as other funding dynamics can be of benefit in the campaign. Certainly knowing about them in advance will encourage campaigners to build the relationship groundwork for when the time comes—if and when that lull comes, it's a really tight spot to be in, not having prepared. But in any case, there are some techniques worth considering. Gary Ploski, who successfully crowdfunded $15,000 on Kickstarter for his film *Rising Star the Movie*, points out the usefulness of lining up a number of contributors to donate on the first day, to get the ball rolling quickly.[19] He also encourages lining up others to contribute on various days thereafter, to even out and keep the momentum going. Ryan Koo, who crowdfunded $125,000 for his fiction film *Manchild*,[20] makes the recommendation that campaigns should start on Monday and end on Friday.[21] This wouldn't necessarily dawn on a campaigner, but the rationale is that more people are accessing their computers on Monday through Friday, and Friday is payday for some.

Rewards and Perks

The essence of crowdfunding campaigns of technology projects differs significantly from those of arts and social cause projects, and that difference is often reflected in the structure of rewards. While the rewards in arts and social campaigns often include some form of gratitude (perhaps along with more tangible items such as DVDs, CDs, tickets, and so on), technology campaigns tend to focus on selling the end product, preselling the technology in question as part of the rewards. In many ways, crowdfunding of technology products appears as part social networking and part *pretailing* (that is, *pre-e-tailing*) operation, sort of an early-phase eBay meets crowdfunding. Of course, equity crowdfunding is a whole different discussion.

For technology projects, the rewards structure likely anchors around the product line. Taking the campaign for Double Fine Adventure (a gaming project that raised a whopping $3.3 million) as an example, the first-level reward of $15 or more states: "The finished game in all of its awesome glory DRM free. . . ."[22] Aside from the size of the funding raise, showing just how popular this campaign was is the fact that 55 percent of the contributors picked this level! All the levels above add on more extras and swag, such as access to a related documentary, sound tracks from the game, posters, and so on. Interestingly, the third-level reward ($60 or more) was less well received, offering a "PDF version of the Double Fine Adventure Book . . ." as well as rewards from the first two levels. Had the campaign been for a project focused on an animated art book, a much different target audience would have probably snapped up this level. But for gamers, this apparently just wasn't as interesting.

After reviewing the successes and failures of many campaigns, one acquires a sixth sense about what rewards will be well received by the perceived audience of any given campaign. And that's actually one of the best diligence items on the to-do list of anyone intending to run a campaign—review many other related and unrelated campaigns that have completed, analyzing them for what worked well and what didn't. It's actually a fun sociology study as well. At any rate, also quite noteworthy in the Double Fine campaign was that rewards associated with all of the top three funding levels had an element of exclusivity (a very limited number offered) and sold out. This is often the case on very successful campaigns.

The TikTok/LunaTik campaign, run by Scott Wilson and his design studio, MINIMAL, crowdfunded sleek and well-designed wristwatch bands and docking hardware that were snap-in compatible with the iPod Nano, making for a full-featured wristwatch.[23] This campaign, run in late 2010, really launched crowdfunding into the limelight when it reached nearly a million dollars of funding. It's also a classic example of the pretailing of technology products using crowdfunding. Only the lowest funding level of "$1 or more," catering to the "Every dollar counts" appeal, wasn't targeted at a specific product. And that level attracted hardly anyone. Contributors wanted the goods, and all of their designed-by-professionals sophistication. And again, the highest and most exclusive funding level ($500 in this case) sold out. For some contributors, it's not just about getting the goods but about getting the goods that few others have.

Now, before anyone gets the idea that technology campaigns are the hottest thing going, it's quite interesting that according to data, they are also the least likely to be funded on Kickstarter. But when they do get funded, they often go really big and receive more contributions than any other category. For fun, which categories according to the same data, would you think have the highest chances of funding success? The answer: theater, music, and dance!

In general, the more tangible the product of a campaign, the more tangible the rewards demanded. The less tangible, the higher the bias is toward rewards of gratitude and participation. At a more macrolevel, the underlying principle is fairness, the true facilitator of all well-functioning transparent markets as well as the basis for common law (a millennia-old concept). Besides the obvious, that a given reward ought to be of interest to the contributor, it's absolutely essential that a potential contributor perceives fairness in the value exchange for the associated rewards. For pretailing, this generally means that there must be a fair deal to the purchaser. Now, goods may be offered at a discount, an obvious value to the purchaser and certainly an indicator of a fair bargain. But a case can also be made for retaining fairness even at a premium. To early adopters, they often find extra value in having first dibs on new or exclusive products. And to many others, at least part of the value exchange comes from the participation in the story.

In all cases, a perception of fairness must be maintained. If, for example, a campaign asked for money to create and sell an exciting new smartphone widget, but the larger vision was for the campaigner to capitalize on the product without returning value to the contributors, social norms would dictate a lack of fairness, and that campaign would likely be poorly funded. No amount of gratitude unbinds the social contract. But if in a campaign for the production of the exact same widget, the expressed goal was stated to be "to donate all profits to put a dying technology whizz-kid on the space shuttle," the campaign may receive massive funding. Even for a technology start-up issuing equity crowdfunding, "5 percent goes toward putting Jamie in orbit" offers a significant advantage vis-à-vis similar competition without. Social value is value. This makes it very hard to generalize many rules about reward structures, other than to say that there needs to be perceived fairness and a proper exchange of value.

Especially in the last decade, VC had its own financial engineering crisis. Whereas the banksters were busy engaging in activities associated with toxic derivatives, high-frequency trading, rehypothetication, extreme leverage, and other forms of wealth extraction, VC's "innovation" was in engineering toxic deal terms. As the VC industry's rate of return continued plummeting after the technology stock IPO bubble burst, rather than adapt along the path of the marketplace, they added heavier-handed terms, which effectively extracted more value from entrepreneurs. This broke the social contract, and it was perceived by many as largely unfair. In the 2000s, many entrepreneurs checked out of the VC hotel for good. A personal friend returned from a discussion with Silicon Valley area VCs about deal terms and reported, "I can't take this anymore. I told them f*** you!" The commoditization of Internet and mobile technologies opened many doors for bootstrapping start-ups to get operational without professional money. And thus, VCs slit their own throats. As long as crowdfunding remains decentralized (that is, not controlled) and transparent, fairness will reign. While it should go without saying, the "happy buyer meets happy seller" equation requires that both parties be happy.

There are, however, some observations from analysis of crowd-funding campaigns and from successful campaigners themselves that are quite useful when applied in an à la carte fashion:

1. For those campaigners who have impressive skills, offering access to time with the campaigner can be a powerful reward, especially with up-and-coming people in the same field. But also to general fans. Who wouldn't want to spend time with their favorite filmmaker?

2. If each higher level of rewards builds on the one below (*cumulative strategy*), it's easier for people to understand, and it builds a more congruous sense of fairness.

3. Both big and small contributors should be captured if possible. Even if people can contribute only a small amount, that drives a sense of commitment to help spread the word about the campaign. There are things that can be offered for only $1, like an mp3 audio file. This needs to be balanced by your ability to execute on and follow up with low-price incentives.

4. If buying a number of items makes sense, higher levels can provide a volume discount (for example, 1 for $50, 2 for $90), which offers a financial incentive.

5. Exclusivity of high-end offerings can be very effective if there is real perceived value. Examine many of the campaigns to get examples of how to frame them.

6. Offering rewards that trigger after a certain amount of funding is reached creates incentives for existing contributors to keep energizing the campaign.

7. The fate of the campaign is highly correlated with the traction it gets in the first week. So get the rewards and the pitch right before coming out of the gates. Get feedback immediately, and adapt if needed.

8. Statistically, 90 percent of a project's funding ends after week 9, and those with tighter timelines tend to convey a sense of commitment and urgency. Plan accordingly.

9. Since its inception, the average funding goal on Kickstarter has risen from $5,000 to $11,000. For financial return crowd-funding, over 80 percent of campaigns raised above $25,000.[24] To get above average raises, it's not a bad idea to be confident that there is above average value offered.

10. In every category except technology, chances of funding suc-cess are much higher if the creator had a success in the past. Apparently in technology, contributors focus more on the goods.

11. In the technology category, the campaigns tend to focus very little on the campaigners and more on the technology.

12. The importance of the locality of the contributors of the campaign is higher at the beginning of the campaign, and it diminishes over time. Thus offering rewards options that require locality to redeem can be more effective than it may seem, especially since those early contributors are quite important.

13. The propensity of more distant contributors to invest in a project rises as a campaign accumulates capital, whereas the propensity of local investors does not.[25]

Choice of the rewards structure needs to be decided not only on the value offered to contributors but even more certainly on the ability to execute on promises. Traditional financing is based on *financial credit* and various metrics that are mostly known by financial institutions and utilities companies. Crowdfunding is a much different animal. While various forms of it may require many of the same financial diligence elements, inherently it's a *social credit* system. And a person's social credit is known in both offline and online circles, indelibly written into (or shall we say, plastered across) the Internet. As the *Crowd Funding Industry Research* report shows, "The same people who were borrowing to consolidate debt had a much lower default rate on crowdfunding platforms, where the crowd has high expectations and is watching, than they did with their initial institutionally funded credit lines."[26]

While crowdfunding is an excellent opportunity to build social credit, one of the things that trips up excited entrepreneurs of all types is poor planning of finances and personal bandwidth. It's not that contributors generally expect that a project will come in exactly on time or budget (unless of course either of those has some extra criticality), or for that matter that things go exactly according to plan (if they do, you'd be one of the few). But there *should* be a plan, demonstrating that the homework and thought process have been done—that's part of the social contract.

An excellent case study of expenditures, after campaign success, is well summarized in the title alone of the article "Less Than a Third of Kickstarter Funds Went on Developing Star Command, Admits War Balloon." In a candid update to their backers, six months after closing a campaign of $37,000, they reported how the money was spent:

> Starting with the absences of $2,000 from no-shows, KickStarter and Amazon Payments naturally took their fill, leaving the developer with $32,000. A further $10,000 went on prize fulfillment, which included printing posters and T-shirts and shipping them globally. In regards to the remaining $22,000, War Balloon spent $6,000 on game music; $4,000 on attorneys, start-up fees, and CPA; $2,000 on poster art; $1,000 on iPads; and $3,000 on attending PAX East. That left the studio with $6,000 to actually finish the game itself—combined with music costs, that's 32 percent of the total pledged.[27]

Actually, quite a few campaigners report being surprised by the time and costs involved in fulfilling reward promises. The great news is that for nearly any kind of project, there is a wealth of people who have done something similar, and they are often quite open about their experiences (especially if they used crowdfunding). Given the reach and accessibility of all forms of social networking, there really are few excuses not to know. Do the homework, do the networking, and do the math in advance. The social credit score very much depends on it.

Chapter | 8

THE JOURNEY

Often the search proves more profitable than the goal.
—E. L. Konigsburg[1]

The future will be an awkward time for control freaks. Perhaps there was a time when linear or rigid thinking yielded something resembling competence or success. But that time has long since passed. This is a bittersweet transition in our cultural history. It's bitter for those people who thrive on rigid planning and checklists and who still leaf through their circa *Leave It to Beaver*[2] business school textbooks for operating procedure. But it's pretty sweet for those who never were really any good at planning ahead of time—everything is changing so fast it wouldn't have been that productive anyway. Just kidding—sort of.

In many fields, including biology, technology, business, and even education, we have conventionally designed and engineered tools and processes that are purposely built to achieve particular goals. But in many other fields, the design cycle is limited by the human engineering element, which poses barriers to scaling the rate of progress of those tools. In an excellent 2009 talk about innovation, as part of Stanford's Entrepreneurial Thought Leader Speaker Series, Steve Jurvetson (partner at Draper Fisher Jurvetson) discussed a trend toward using artificial evolution to accelerate the rate of progress.[3] He referred to the example of the company Genomatica, which wanted to modify organisms to convert sugars to a desired chemical. After initially creating such an organism, using purposeful (human engineered) design, they were able to tweak the organism to obtain a 20-fold improvement in the amount of the desired chemical produced. But using an artificial evolution technique of repeatedly skimming off more productive organisms to create newer more efficient batches, they obtained a 20,000-fold improvement thereafter.

When relating this example to a conceptually similar quote from the computer science book *The Pattern on the Stone*, Jurvetson really put the crosshairs on the target when he stated: "I think it's the future of complex systems development in general, that the design-engineered purposeful approach is going to cede way to more of an out-of-control biologic process in both the literal sense and in the metaphorical sense in how we build systems of software." Now, this may seem a bit "too techie" for some at first, until it's realized that he just described the way that social networking works, the way social graphs are formed, the way new information traverses and is digested by participants on the Internet, and so on. In this case, *we* are the organisms. And the system is our new economy.

All new information that enters the system, changes the system. Sometimes the impact of a piece of information is less significant. But imagine if tomorrow it was discovered that Facebook is really a front group for an alien race collecting information for its plan to make soylent green out of us all. Much of the entire social graph of the Internet would change in 24 hours, based on this one new piece of information. While that may be a science-fiction example to make the point, the reality is that our social web is essentially a living, breathing organism constantly taking in new information. And we live in a veritable sea of new information and change. Your business model will change, your customers will change, your product will change, and your traction will change. And certainly a crowdfunding campaign needs to adapt. It should be treated a lot less like an event and more like a journey.

Follow Inspiration with Massive Action

As Thomas Edison said, "What it boils down to is 1 percent inspiration and 99 percent perspiration." Or put in a more modern and related crowdfunding context: "Inspire people to be part of your dream, what with high integrity and authenticity, and then just take massive action,"[4] a powerful missive from Chris Jones, author of *The Guerilla Film Makers Handbook*.[5] There aren't many worthwhile achievements in life that come easily, and certainly running a campaign is no exception. Not surprisingly, many people who run campaigns report that doing so is at least a part-time if not a full-time job. It nearly has to be that way. While portals make crowdfunding incredibly accessible, let's not forget that the same accessibility is available to everyone else as well—just as many people are in the same boat in terms of needing capital and other resources, and a number of them will also surface campaigns and compete for a share of the collective attention (and money). The more successful and popular a portal becomes, the more it will draw even more people to use it. And thus, competition for resources is ramped up significantly. Open systems have a way of maintaining a natural balance.

Seemingly, this would put a potential campaigner back to square 1, in the never-ending struggle to stay afloat. This perspective is misguided, and it can be seen in reports of frustration from people who have run less-than-successful campaigns. Without doubt, most proper campaigns require a lot of planning and work, as well they should. Otherwise, "the market" would step in and quickly rebalance the equation. Rather, many unsuccessful campaigns disconnect on one or more levels. A classic mistake that many of them make is to do the initial work, launch a campaign, and send out a news blast, and then they wait for the campaign to "go viral." That kind of fire can easily burn out as quickly as it's started. Until the discovery of Crowdfunding Elves who quietly find interesting campaigns and then diligently spread the message while campaigners go on about their lives, we're on our own. Campaigns are a relationship-building and storytelling process. This takes time and energy to develop. And of course, significant value of some form has to be offered.

People who try to "get" value are generally wasting their time and energy. Those who endeavor to develop value, build platforms for future development. Don't fight this. Embrace it—it's nature's eternal gift to us, a veritable "screw you" to ward off sociopathic "taker" behavior. What's often at play with campaigns that don't get the traction they desire is that the campaigners don't have the right equation. If they have an interesting story that resonates with an appropriately sized audience and they are able to reach out to that audience, then generally good things happen. If they haven't developed the story or they haven't developed the relationships that allow them to reach an interested audience, then their only hope is that a fire starts by serendipity—perhaps some random person will step in and stoke the fire for them. A campaign may get some arbitrary traffic from the natural discovery process on a portal (people searching, browsing, or looking at the most popular projects page). But as Danae Ringelmann, founder of Indiegogo, asserts, "It's not the engine."[6] You and your relationship network are the engine. It's best to consider portals as facilitation mechanisms. Everything else that they can bring is a bonus.

Keep the fire lit, and continuously deliver value to the crowd. If being part of your story is of value, then keeping supporters updated with interesting parts of the story delivers value. After successful funding is reached, likely an even greater part of your story awaits. The great news in all of this is that if one accepts crowdfunding as a process of development, participation, and feedback, rather than an event, then it encourages getting started earlier than later. Rather than overanalyzing, overplanning, and waiting for perfection, it's often better to get something out there and start the feedback process. Getting a rough video pitch in front of friends, for example, can garner a lot of rapid feedback on things you never thought of. Polishing that a little and then getting it in front of a targeted audience can yield powerful further feedback. Whenever you can handle the exposure, iteration with rapid-fire feedback has shown to produce results. In the open source realm, this mentality was codified with the oft-repeated mantra, "Release early and often." When you pour heart and integrity into storytelling and building relationships, people will forgive you for some of your imperfections. They may well identify with you more and want to be part of your story.

Drive Traffic with Social Networking

Once you get over 50 percent of the funding, you have a 90 percent chance of reaching your goal, according to filmmaker Meg Pinsonneault, founder of Thirsty Girl Films.[7] That's good news that turns into better news, if you know how you got to the first 50 percent! Even better yet, ask other people how they got there before you get started. Given a fixed amount of hours in the day and a relatively fixed number of people on the team, it's critical to focus the campaign spot beam where it's most effective. As was mentioned, the campaign often turns into either a part-time or full-time job, which can surprise the uninitiated. There are so many other diversions (and campaigns) for would-be contributors to contend with that it often takes a continual push to keep the momentum going.

Part of the homework of running a campaign is to "get smart" quickly on the latest social networking and analytics tools (or of course you can get friendly with someone who is really savvy about those things). The tools du jour may change, but what remains the same is that asking other campaigners what worked can provide a treasure trove of information, including things that are specific to your target market. And, hey, if they're part of a "Kicking It Forward" program (like the Kickstarter-specific honor-system program with that name, whereby participants pledge to put 5 percent of the finished product profits back into other projects), maybe they'll feel compelled to contribute.[8] In any case, here's a list of some common tools to get familiar with. Pick the tools that make the most sense to your project:

1. Have as many links as possible go to the campaign blog and other related pages. This way people don't get distracted off site, and the platform analytics gather data.
2. Platforms often provide custom (shortened) referral website addresses that tie into their analytics. Use those.
3. Add a campaign link to e-mail signature and chat status.
4. Send personal e-mails with a direct ask to your friends and colleagues.
5. Make frequent Facebook status updates.
6. Add links to videos (YouTube, Vimeo, and others).
7. Annotate YouTube videos with campaign links making it easy for users to get to your campaign.
8. Use Google Analytics and Vimeo statistics.
9. Update Twitter, Flickr, and LinkedIn profiles with links to the campaign.
10. Considering tying your campaign updates to your Twitter and other social networking accounts.
11. Use campaign widgets (provided by the platform) on blogs and websites.

12. Use LinkedIn Groups and LinkedIn Answers features.
13. Post information about the campaign on Facebook walls of related organizations.
14. Revitalize any mailing lists that you have already.
15. Respond to comments and questions on the campaign site and on any other social networks.
16. Provide updates to the current contributors and campaign pages.
17. Use Twitter search to find out about users' activities related to the campaign (there are some third-party search engines that are quite good).
18. Use Google news and blogs search. Also, set news triggers on your project for daily updates.
19. Use any other share tool that makes sense.

Of course, that's only a small cross-section of the online social networking presence one can have. But much of social networking doesn't occur on the Internet. Make up some business cards for the campaign and perhaps fliers and other materials (song samples, video clips, pictures of a prototype, and so on). Have them at the ready for the relentless assault (meant affectionately) at trade events, conferences, social events, mixers, meetups, parties, random elevator encounters, flash mobs, and whatever else you do. The work of an entrepreneur is never over.

Motivate Your Network: Keep Them Involved

For those contributors operating in the conventional "board of directors" mode of venture finance, once-monthly financial and progress updates might make them all warm and tingly inside. For the rest, the idea is that they bought a ticket to participate in your journey. Keep them updated and excited to be part of it. The Double Fine Adventure project team did something really cool—they made a multi-episode documentary about the making of the game, which they provided to backers. Way before the end product was ready, gamers and other contributors were already receiving value. Those are going to be some loyal fans! It's hard to find a more polar opposite from classic Silicon Valley "stealth mode" than that. It would be great to see this trend catch on in many categories. And for those few gamers on Earth who apparently didn't fund Double Fine, no worries as the website states: "It's never too late for ADVENTURE!" You can pay $15 through PayPal, and you're in.[9]

For most projects, there's value that can be delivered in the interim. For some, the story behind making the story is a story of its own. Creators of an application might release prototypes to backers, or they might run a logo contest. Filmmakers might release video clips, or they might invite contributors to film shoots—maybe put contributors in as extras. An urban farmer might invite people to help break ground. And so on. Generally, people are far more apt to contribute if there is more immediate feedback. Even something small can be an attractor—you don't necessarily have to live in a fishbowl to keep people entertained. Something now and something later generally beats something later.

Above all, send heartfelt gratitude to contributors, in a way that's unique to your team and project. And of course, one of the ultimate forms of gratitude is turning contributions into something real.

PART | III

THE ROAD AHEAD

In today already walks tomorrow.
—Friedrich von Schiller

Chapter | 9

INFRASTRUCTURE
AND ECOSYSTEMS

If there's an ecosystem where things are free,
your currency becomes enthusiasm.
—Frank Chimero

As the crush of macroforces squeezes the old-school venture financing industry, the potential of crowdfunding accelerates, seemingly balanced by financing's analog to the first law of thermodynamics. But to even remotely conceptualize or relate the changing landscape of project financing in terms of a zero-sum equation, like the reshuffling of chips from person to person in a poker game, would be to completely misunderstand the entirety of the crowdfunding revolution. What is occurring now and the potentials moving forward are not a result of a singular shift or trend. Rather, the emerging incarnation of crowdfunding is a result of many ongoing socioeconomic trends, including the removal of a number of inefficiencies that have plagued capital allocation for much of our history. It will be accompanied by *force multipliers* derived from modern-day social networking combined with some techniques that are better understood and applied in the financial sector (which we'll elaborate on more in a following chapter).

A zero-sum displacement or disruption of any type of business or trend would imply that there's a balanced shift away from one thing and toward another. What's occurring with crowdfunding has no such symmetry. It's not just replacing one thing with another that is better. Rather, it is enabling and exploiting something far greater. This is best explained in terms of using the "VC industry" as an example. However, before going any further, it's worthwhile to stop for a moment and explain why the quotes were used around "VC industry." While it's a useful literary device to talk about this industry as a single embodiment, it's not very accurate. From the financial performance perspective, it's certainly deceiving to think about the industry as a whole, a point made by Marc Andreessen in a talk he gave at Stanford, summarized by his statements to that effect: "So first of all, I don't believe there is such a thing as the Venture Capital industry," and "I think you've got a set of firms, you've got 20, 30, 40 boutique VC firms that do really well over time, and then you've got about 660 firms that will generally very much break your heart as an investor if you invest in them."[1] Those are points well made. But outside of financial performance, there are other important ways in which the VC industry is incoherent. Let's talk about one of them, VC infrastructure, and then we'll look at the related ecosystems that are really constructs enabled by the VC infrastructure, be they formally and intentionally created or otherwise.

The Power of Virtual Infrastructure

Of course, I'm really only joking when referring to "VC infrastructure." While the industry has its own microcosm of human networks and possibly internal deal flow management software, to the entrepreneur and other ecosystem participants, there is not much by way of common infrastructure gluing individual VC firms together. They have the outward appearance of an archipelago, a string of islands nearing each other but not connected. From the "industry" that gave us Google, Cisco, and Facebook, excepting for perhaps some very new model start-up incubators, there is little e-infrastructure in the industry, exemplified by the following Q&A: Can you write a VC app? Nope. Can you push a button and move your dossier to another VC firm? Nope. Can you easily run some VC analytics? Nope. There isn't just a lack of infrastructure. There is nearly a complete lack of transparency, something that led to the rise of third-party sites like TheFunded,[2] which allows the crowd to rate firms and individual investors, and CrunchBase,[3] which is kind of a wiki for keeping track of important facets of the start-up realm, like funding events.

Think about the potential that has been unlocked each time the general population was given access to a desirable standard such as TCP/IP, API (for example, iPhone, Android), document formats (for example, PDF, XML), and data feeds (for example, Twitter, RSS). It's not just that these things enabled the first-order participants (like iPhone developers targeting the iPhone stack). It's that a whole crop of ecosystem participants can now interact, creating a huge force multiplier. Now consider crowdfunding, which is really at the intersection of social networking and venture financing. Today's crowdfunding is by its very nature a platform, with an innately electronic infrastructure. Therein lies some of the key elements of crowdfunding's immensely constructive (that is, nonzero-sum) potential and hints of the very rich and innovative ecosystem to come.

But as previously explained, an infrastructure isn't some optional "nice-to-have" feature for financing ideas. It's an absolute necessity! As the rate of change marches forward, as well as the globalization of innovation and rapid dispersion of ideas via the Internet, human-to-human networks have absolutely buckled under the volumetric stress. Sorting through an exponentially growing pile is an immense scalability problem. And the investment world's biggest irony is that there are more diamonds than ever to be found—it's just that they're buried in exponentially more roughage! The answer to this scalability problem lies in the power of social networks, ecosystem enablement, and in something discussed in the next chapter, prediction markets, which actually have the opposite scaling characteristics— they scale better with more inputs!

I originally became interested in crowdfunding while thinking through what a small and new-order VC firm would look like if it employed an externally facing crowdfunding and social networking mechanism to solve the early-stage scalability issues. While thinking through the mechanisms involved and the power that such a platform would provide, it became apparent (especially as we move forward) that it may be better to think in terms of the inverse scenario: mapping a VC face onto a crowdfunding platform. Because in a lot of ways, it is the platform, and the connectivity to so many people that it provides, that is the underlying source of value creation. While a number of the platform ideas in this chapter stem from related thinking, at least as many came from "jamming" with my coauthor, Dan, as well as many other crowdfunding-related people we interviewed. This chapter is truly a product of the crowd, or at least from a "core sample" of it.

As people discover crowdfunding, they generally do at least a quick survey of the websites that service the kinds of projects they're interested in—perhaps funding an independent movie, a fashion item, or technology start-up. But the odds are they'll end using a platform that is fairly primitive, simply because most of them are in their early phases of development (excepting for various lending platforms, as many of them have undergone the regulatory gauntlet, sometimes including a period of being shut down, and the business gauntlet, having been around longer than other forms of crowdfunding). Many platforms hue toward the social networking side of the spectrum, but with various crowdfunding facilities added on. To some degree, that's the nature of the fast-paced "release early and often" development paradigm. But the irony is that one of the most sophisticated crowdfunding platforms discovered in our research was one you may never have heard of called OffRoad Capital,[4] and it was founded circa 1997 (and later acquired in 2001 by NYPPe Holdings, Inc.[5]). Well, that is, if you consider an infrastructure that is constrained to a (albeit a very large) network of wealthy investors as crowdfunding. Look at some of the features incorporated into OffRoad Capital's operations:

1. Live webcasts and TV (archived also)
2. Sophisticated best practices
3. Virtual road shows (also archived)
4. Disclosure practices
5. Tools and analytics
6. Standardized quarterly reports (like public companies)
7. Secondary market (liquidity for illiquid markets) access
8. Its own self-regulatory organization (SRO) as part of its company structure
9. Its own licensing platform
10. Third-party access from outsiders like analysts and researchers, much like the access companies in the public equity markets grant to outsiders
11. Other "secret sauce"

One of the members of OffRoad, Steve Cinelli, went on to found PRIMARQ.[6] This platform was even more sophisticated (including advancements in technology such as the use of cloud computing and open source that enabled transactions to be accomplished better, faster, and less expensively) in that it aggregated funding from a large pool of investors for the purpose of funding real estate transactions. These are fantastic reference model platforms that the crowdfunding industry should keep in mind when thinking about future directions of infrastructure and business best practices. And in a lot of ways, they were and are pioneering platforms.

The Ecosystem

There are so many reasons why tomorrow's crowdfunding platforms will need to offer a level of sophistication that can fulfill the needs of a rich ecosystem, that is, it's pretty easy to make the prediction that most of the platforms that will not survive, especially the financial ROI-based ones. In the way that Facebook and Apple have APIs and apps, so too will crowdfunding. Exposing APIs and data is imperative. Even from only a competitive standpoint, it'll be hard to compete for attention (which *is* more of a zero-sum game) when a competitor's platform offers a vibrant and virally adopted ecosystem—a recipe for sucking in participants from more lame platforms. But competitive forces aside, here are a number of considerations that we hope will drive home the point, and then we will look at the potentials of the future crowdfunding platform:

1. Serious, professional investors will require quality infrastructure, best practices, and so on. Note that this is no different in the creative arts production world. For example, in movie making, you do want the *option* for your cheaply made indie movie to get visibility with some larger industry players too, right?
2. Regulators will be a lot more comfortable, as it should be easier to police. More will be discussed about some of the relevant features later on.
3. Third-party analysts and researchers will be able to tap into the platform, much as is done for the public equity marketplace.

By the way, academic researchers might be a good first adopter for whatever (anonymized) data can expose—there is a dearth of start-up information to analyze.

4. Advertising money will migrate toward the highest-value platforms.

5. Fraud prevention algorithms will need good infrastructure. Note that algorithms can do some of work for us, given the high volume of early-phase projects.

6. Analytics and trend analysis will be high-value items to many parties. Without good infrastructure, there can't be good analytics.

7. To service a large base of people on a given platform, it will be critical that the platform play the part of the matchmaker, much like a dating service. Without the matchmaking capability, what would be an otherwise successful crowdfunding platform will be a victim of its own success. When there are too many participants, there is seemingly too much noise. It's critical to have intelligent filtering mechanisms to make people's lives easier. This is one form of algorithmic curation, people and organizations being the other.

Now then, let's dive into the future crowdfunding platform and discuss some of the challenges that it faces. A career as a many-time entrepreneur and software architect type has taught a discipline of starting at the end point and working backward, thinking through how to get to that end point from where we are now. In that spirit, proposed are many of the aspects of future crowdfunding platforms that in turn we believe will give birth to the next socioeconomic revolution.

Realizing much of the full platform potential from the onset is critical. It's critical because it will empower people with ideas to design more meaningful crowdfunding platforms. It will also help create a vision for policy makers and regulators who would like to help their countries achieve a competitive and rich economic boom—and regulators and policy makers are major participants in this evolving crowdfunding story.

If one were to apply taxonomy to crowdfunding, the high-level supertypes might include creative arts and entertainment, conventional Venture Capital, peer-to-peer lending, and philanthropy. But the life of a crowdfunding taxonomist would be quite frustrating. Not only because in reality there are so many crowdfunding niches that would need to be put in their proper place in the taxonomic organization chart (where do we put crowdfunding of next year's wine by selling wine futures?), not only because some sites allow crowdfunding across many species of projects (Indiegogo calls out the following on its site: "Art, Music, Gaming, Design, Film, Writing, Technology, Photography, Invention, Venture, Green, Food, Political, Education, Community, Performing Arts"[7]), but also because it's actually possible to combine various styles of crowdfunding for a given project.

In fact, it's not just possible to do so. It's also necessary. We believe it's very important to combine styles of crowdfunding, to fully catalyze the full social dynamics that empower the crowdfunding model. We therefore predict that hybridization will become commonplace. Subsequent discussion will elaborate on that, but for now, a key observation from studying crowdfunding is that if one sets aside the "personality" or particulars of a given crowdfunding site, much of the infrastructure, memes, social networking dynamics, and best practices are quite similar in nature or at least have very strong parallels. For the purposes of this chapter's discussion, we picked a financial return (that is, a "micro-VC") bent because it's sort of the highest-common-denominator case, meaning that it has some very high expectations from the participants who use it.

Well, the first thing that's obvious about the future crowdfunding platform is that it must do a fantastic job acting as a dating service (that is, matchmaker) for all the participants. If some current crowdfunding platforms seem to be enjoying a level of "success" (and, by the way, for a number of them, that's not tied in any way to a performance metric other than their having received funding), it's out of scarcity. Imagine for a moment that every poor person on the African continent requested funding on Kiva! This would overwhelm the pool of potential funders and create a very different (and dissuasive) dynamic.

Scarcity can often mask the lack of capacity to handle scalability. This scarcity currently characterizes the state of affairs in which much of crowdfunding currently lives, but less so each and every day. It's quite possible that, for a time, many people will get saturated with crowdfunding until various forms of curation take over the saturating load and bandwidth of and increasing number of available campaigns. It may take time before infrastructure and social behaviors mature to catch up with the volume. The online dating industry has lived through its own transition from scarcity to abundancy, and it figured out how to navigate this dynamic a long time ago. As a result, it does a lot of matchmaking for the participants. People can search at will all they want, but mostly people let the matchmaking search criteria do at least some of the work. To search through the entire database would be an untenable proposition, at least for a human anyway.

The Power of Tags

But matchmaking isn't confined to people with money to invest or donate and those looking to receive funding. To get to any scale, a platform must enable a whole ecosystem of participants. The platform must help match cofounders and employees, lawyers, accountants, graphics designers, PR firms, outsourcing firms, and so on—everybody and anybody—each person having one or more roles. So it's very important that the platform understand the various personas that each participant acts under. It must also understand geolocation, languages, sectors, technologies involved, for-profit versus nonprofit status, ages, and just about every facet one can imagine. This would at first blush seem untenable at best, if not nearly impossible at worst, given that the universe of things that may become interesting is hard to know until it becomes interesting (and that seems to happen in real time these days).

But it's not so bad. Enter the *tag cloud* and the social networking dynamics that facilitate it. Even better yet would be to think of a *key-value-pair cloud*, but that sounds so much less sexy. The difference is that a tag has only very limited dimensionality ("iPhone" versus "Android"), whereas adding further quantitative and qualitative dimension ("rating: 68 percent" or "fuel: biodiesel") allows for much more intelligent search capabilities, and the crowd would have a way to more sensibly rank, categorize, and otherwise structure things, without the infrastructure imposing any particular structure a priori. Anyway, let's refer to these generically as *tags*.

Tags are the oil lubricating the social dynamics machinery of the future and especially so for crowdfunding. We can see them already hard at work in many instances online, such as in the Twitter hashtags, in Flickr, and in blogs. But they'll be absolutely critical for crowdfunding if it's to reach its potentially huge scale. Why? Well, first because the way to handle the scaling issue of funding early-phase projects is to use the scale of the crowd by empowering it. Fight fire with fire, or at least scale with scale. It's imperative to continually tap into the collective wisdom of the crowd, and to do that we need a mechanism to allow the crowd to make small (and by small we mean *really* small) contributions.

If you've ever looked at the statistics from many online sites, you're aware that in reality most users tend to merely consume content, be they watching a YouTube video or reading a *Wikipedia* article. Generally only a tiny percentage of users actually actively create content. As articulated in Clay Shirky's book *Here Comes Everybody*: "Fewer than 2 percent of *Wikipedia* users ever contribute, yet that is enough to create profound value for millions of users."[8] What's more intriguing is the viral power of even the most simplistic initial *stub* (a placeholder for more substantial content). Shirky provides the amusing example of the progression of the *Wikipedia* article on "Asphalt." The initial stub read, in full: "Asphalt is a material used for road coverings."[9] Merely the existence of the stub allows the "article" to show up under search, which attracts attention, which then ultimately attracts contributions to the article, and so on. Translated to crowdfunding, stubs are the initial creation of a tag, and editing correlates to further qualifying or quantifying a tag.

Tags are, in some ways, the least amount of active effort a user can impart, and as alluded to, it's really important to keep the expectations of user inputs low (the crowd's "having a handful of highly motivated people and a mass of barely motivated ones"[10]). Yet with such a simplistic facility, the collective crowd can describe the infinitely complex, dynamic, and multidimensional structure of projects that exist on a given platform at any one point in time, all without requiring any preconceived notion of structure a priori, by the platform.

So let's say that a given project seeking funds adds a minimal amount of tags. And those match on some searches of other participants, enough to attract at least one of them to add another relevant tag, which attracts more participants who add more tags. If incentivized to tag properly (tip jar, credits, and so on), the dynamics can help seed the tag cloud, which is extremely useful for matchmaking, other search motivations, and some other activities (which we'll cover later). It's very helpful to know the age and number of eyeballs that have vetted a given tag, which then helps with an evaluation of the tag's validity, especially if arbitrary people are contributing. It's a bit metaphoric, but we can call this *tag viscosity* because in the beginning a new tag is very fluid, but it can become much firmer over time after enough vetting has taken place. And for what it's worth, if trends reverse and a tag should become out-moded, there's no reason it can't phase back to fluidity or dissipate altogether.

So what can we do with our tag cloud? Imagine that there are currently 1 million start-up pitches on a given crowdfunding site. Let's affectionately call the website the contrived name FundHarmony (a play on the hybridization of the word *fund*ing and the dating site *eHarmony*.com). Without any form of intelligent matching, a would-be funder that logs in might experience that sensation of being caught in the middle of a stampede. But instead, FundHarmony presents them with an initial and sensible match of various participants, displaying, "We believe you may be interested in funding these 10 start-ups" or "You'd be a great cofounder in these 5 start-ups that are looking for someone like you" or "The following VCs would like your expert opinion of the following potential start-ups," and so on. This is possible by matching the user-supplied information to the many inputs from the crowd, including tags. FundHarmony is already something larger than crowdfunding. It's actually a social networking site based on the matchmaking of participants in the field of crowdfunding. And it's already underway toward becoming tomorrow's mechanism for finding jobs. But this is just the beginning.

Integration and Evolution in the Ecosystem

A very common way to pitch an idea online is to make a video. Videos make it easy, on a human level, to get familiar with the people behind the idea or cause, and they are far easier to digest than reading through a PowerPoint presentation. There's no particular reason that a project should be confined to a single video presentation. If the project creators were so inclined, they could post periodic video "check-ins" and talk about their work-in-progress idea, promote some inputs from their fan base, and discuss their progress toward funding goals. Potentially, video check-ins could be recorded in real time and broadcast out live (and archived), thereby creating a mini-TV series that drives the stickiness and virality of their project. And why should they stop after getting funding? These kinds of podcasts have become an integrated part of their marketing strategy. So the FundHarmony platform creates partnerships with video infrastructure companies. Of course, it would be great to have the video and audio searchable, or in a form that can be e-mailed or tweeted out. Fortunately, with a large base of users descending on the problem, many of the fans can be incentivized to transcribe audio tracks to text, and they can further translate them to other languages, wherever computer transcription and translation fails. To a degree, crowdfunding is absorbing the "reality TV" theme, and thus the related market.

As the process of fund-raising—and in fact, an increasing amount of the life cycle of a project—goes online, it becomes evident that the traditional role of a board of directors (BOD) has become clunky, if not anachronistic. While some start-ups continue requiring the tight control of information afforded by a BOD, to protect company secrets, many new-order start-ups and other types of projects have found that transparency returns more in the upside from the social networking dynamics than it exposes in the downside. By offering postfunding facilitation mechanisms such as online financial reporting (all of the start-up's finances are now imported into the project's crowdfunding account), contract accountants (who have become members on FundHarmony) now perform financial oversight. There is also artificial intelligence (AI) logic on the platform that conducts algorithmic anomaly and fraud detection. Given the existing video and document reporting infrastructure, adding a voting mechanism to FundHarmony's infrastructure enables a new shift to occur. Investors subsume the role of the board of directors—they become one and the same. One share, one vote. Who was overseeing the board before, anyway?

Most people in the world are pretty busy, and investors are no different. Fortunately a healthy ecosystem (a marketplace, if you will) allows people to trade off things they have in abundance for things they lack. Jane Dollars has a lot of money to invest on FundHarmony, but her schedule is jam packed. Fortunately, she got connected via FundHarmony to Johnny Onthespot, who just graduated with heaps of student loans, and he has a graduate degree in biotechnology. Johnny has this uncanny ability to sort through the pitches in his field of study, and he finds the absolute best and most fundable start-ups.

Recognizing this kind of dynamic early on, FundHarmony added the concept and infrastructure for a *finder*: a third party who can facilitate and take over matchmaking where social networking and AI fall short. Johnny has begun paying off his school debt from finders' fees, and he works as a finder for 10 different investors, for whom he customizes finding activities, based on their profiles and private interactions. He can choose to take fees up front or share in the potential returns from the start-ups he facilitates funding for, thanks to insightful regulators who understood that allowing third parties into the equation would be an enormous force multiplier for the economic engine that is crowdfunding.

But matching with funders is only one kind of activity that is facilitated by finders. Finders can also match up lawyers, employees (finders can be the new "headhunters"), graphics designers, and so on. The rise of finders has become its own revolution, and it has created a new "finders' economy," which I've previously written about in my blog post "The Coming Finders' Economy: Intermediation of Life Online."[11] And FundHarmony is becoming an entire and rich ecosystem that is part of that revolution.

It was inevitable: as the enormity of FundHarmony grew, the next tier of ecosystem players joined in. They demanded more extensive APIs and data mining capabilities (properly anonymized and with customer-friendly optionality, of course), but they were willing to pay higher premium monthly account fees to get such access. The site now offers a whole new spectrum of professional analysis, analytics, trend reporting, and forecasts for start-ups, which include those from the indie entertainment and fashion industries, among many others. Private equity firms, VC firms, corporations, sovereign wealth funds, and many other classes of investors are paying for this research, to help them decide where to allocate early-stage capital. Hollywood spends an increasing amount of time sourcing deals and talent using the site. The influx of these new participants is pushing the growth rate of FundHarmony to the technological limits of the platform (which is otherwise known in the start-up world as a "quality problem").

Recognizing that there is always room for combining the new power of the crowdfunding platform with an especially bright and knowledgeable boutique of partners, a new order of crafty venture capitalists create a firm that funds only crowdfunded plays. They tap into the search and screening facilities offered by FundHarmony, but what's more, they combine access to it via APIs with their own networks, wisdom, and external data, which they believe gives them an edge over the competition. But the same idea occurred to some bright people who used to work at black-box hedge funds. Their external information is sourced differently, but their network of mathematics and economics PhDs believes it's not necessary to come from the venture industry to outperform the market, now that this rich new ecosystem exists. Some identify trends early and jump on funding opportunities quickly. Others specialize on finding what is being underfunded. There really are no shortages of investment strategies.

When Dartboards Are Better Than Groupthink

Departing from my futuristic storyline for a quick interlude, those black-box folks may well be correct. In my research, I got a chance to talk with Right Side Capital,[12] a new seed-stage investment firm with an interesting new twist. The company found in its own research, based on analysis runs using a database of real, historical seed-stage data, that if a firm can do a first-order screen of potential seed deals based on some simple scoring, then it can produce respectable returns by funding a random sample of start-ups, as long as the sample size is large enough (Right Side Capital's site states: "100 to 200 seed investments per year. Investment decisions in two weeks"[13]). I like to joke that the company should be called "Dartboard Capital." Though a little humorous, it's unfortunately not surprising.

Along with many of the other reasons mentioned in this book regarding the sad state of affairs that is Venture Capital, some of this can be attributed to the groupthink phenomena that pervades many panels of people, be they partners at VC firms or angel syndicates or some other type of investment brokerages. And this is well illustrated by the following anecdotal comment from a private conversation with a past VC: "Before any of the other partners voiced a strong opinion, we always looked out of the corner of our eyes to see what the lead partner was thinking." This evokes the sentiment of a line from Jeff Howe's book *Crowdsourcing*: "If great minds think alike—and in many circumstances they do—then they really constitute only one mind."[14] Note to LPs: you're paying some really steep management fees for having only one mind.

At any rate, if a random number generator can do a better job than many VC firms or angel syndicates, than one can assume that a few black-box funds will figure out how to gain an advantage from intelligence.

Funding the Way the Market Wants It

Now then, back to the future. The crowdfunding phenomenon has not been the only ongoing change occurring in the start-up realm. The very lumpy and distortive discrete-round-of-funding model has been incrementally replaced by the *rolling close*, whereby start-ups take money from investors incrementally until they feel they have enough. This was a change adopted and explained years prior by Y Combinator's Paul Graham.[15] This means of funding turned out to be highly advantageous to the entrepreneur "because it requires less reliance on a lead investor, takes less time out of product development, and gives investors less room to drag things along or collude."[16]

While it took the VC industry over 60 years to adopt this new model, it took only a few days to integrate it into the FundHarmony platform. What's more, the whole concept of rounds of funding has all but disappeared, as any particular start-up or project is, at any point in time, either looking to raise more money or not. What sense did it ever make to have names for rounds of funding or a prescribed progression of funding requirements? It's possible for a project to live month to month, getting funding nearly in real time. While that sounds a little frightening at first, if there is more demand for a popular start-up than there is equity supply in exchange, it actually turns out to be a no-brainer (thanks to well-functioning open markets), and it results in founders who retain a far bigger percentage of their company.

Unfortunate as it may be, many of the old-school venture firms were reactive instead of proactive, and therefore they didn't make the switch in time. Perhaps they should have adopted Paul Graham's thinking, exemplified by his prescient statement in a *TechCrunch* video interview: "If you want to be an investor ahead of your time, just figure out how founders would like you to behave and start doing that now."[17]

Deal terms used to be a dark art in the start-up world. For a while, it seemed like each deal had attached to it an increasing number of caustic ways for VCs to extract further value and control from start-ups, while accepting less of the risk. But this school of thinking was a nonstarter in crowdfunding, where transparency, scalability, and natural market forces reign. Outside of crowdfunding, there were several efforts to open source deal terms for seed and series A stages.[18] Much of the essence of these efforts was quickly imported into the FundHarmony platform and converted to a simple-to-use point-and-click interface for creating deal contracts. The dark art of trying to game performance by "deal terms engineering" dissipated, and the focus returned to finding the best start-up opportunities that produced the most real value.

Solving the Hoarding Dilemma

Of course, convincing entrepreneurs who believe they have high-value ideas to list their pitch on a public crowdfunding platform runs contrary to basic human instincts, which tend to drive people to hoard their proprietary insights. Outside of regulatory issues, this was one of the main forms of resistance to the crowdfunding paradigm early on in the game. And it was a quite rational response, given the historical environment for start-ups. But aside from needed regulatory reform in the intellectual property space, all it took was the launching of a high-value start-up using crowdfunding to set the stage for a cultural shift in entrepreneurial spirits.

A couple of college kids had a brilliant idea, during some downtime in between classes and keg parties. They invented a way to predict what a person would search for in advance, and they thought the timing was right to drop out of college and build a start-up called Fuugle, which they affectionately derived from the word *future* and the name of the search leviathan *Google*. This was way better than real-time search. This was *before*-time search, kind of like breaking the temporal sound barrier of search! As the market capitalization of this kind of start-up certainly would reach $1 quadrillion, they had initial reservations about creating an account and putting their pitch online for all to see. Who wouldn't?

But the founders of FundHarmony had realized early on that going big meant attracting the creators of the next hottest thing to use their platform to launch. All it would take is one big win using FundHarmony, and history would be written. After many false starts and a lot of head-scratching on a new way to solve the issues surrounding the hoarding dilemma, the FundHarmony founders had had an epiphany. Why change anything? Why not just re-create the natural human relationship and trust building schemes, but online? Well, it was either an epiphany or what some call the "Duh! moment."

After interviewing a number of entrepreneurs and other start-up players, they quickly divined the common mechanisms that were at play in the "song and dance" that is relationship and trust building. Simply put, in the beginning an entrepreneur exposes very little "surface area" of the big idea to a relatively bigger audience. Over time, there is a lot more exposure to a very small audience, each of whom the entrepreneur has screened as a potential fit and with whom he or she has developed some sense of trust. Well, this is really the same dynamic that goes on in most any kind of relationship building.

Illustrated in Figure 9.1, this looks like two directionally opposite pyramids or funnels. As the number of participants in one funnel narrows, the amount of trust per remaining participant in the other funnel increases. FundHarmony thus needed the mechanisms to enable that natural progression to occur, after which the human nature of the crowdfunding platform users would do the rest. FundHarmony went about implementing features to enable this, and it was not only well accepted but in some ways it also empowered the crowdfunding members even more. It allowed a greater scale than human-to-human networking could ever achieve. Let's look at what and why.

FundHarmony allowed entrepreneurs to enter or upload an arbitrary sequence of information that could be exposed to

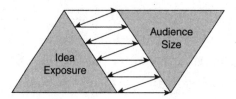

Figure 9.1 Human-to-Human Networking

funders—everything from a one-line pitch to a paragraph pitch to an executive summary to a full-on business plan. (I once heard of an investor who actually reads these!) Ditto for videos and other forms of media. At every stage of disclosure by a given potential funding party, the entrepreneur can define a gating mechanism. This mechanism can be manual (override), programmatic (simple Boolean logic or a full script language), or automatic (preset logic or scripts) in whatever ways it guides or blocks a party in the progression.

The same gating mechanism can be used for information flow or for other purposes such as determining who can contact a given entrepreneur in the first place. The offline method of trust building would be conceptually identical to setting all gatings to "manual." Or perhaps the gates could be set to something like, "Only pass through people who know my first-order circle." Or if you're a fan of TheFunded.com, perhaps you set your gates to, "Don't allow contact from VCs who have a rating of less than 3.5." In fact, over time FundHarmony had created value above TheFunded. Beyond letting the crowd rate VCs, it would actually know how they performed financially, how early they arrived on the scene, and much more.

After learning of the sophisticated and entrepreneur-friendly mechanisms that FundHarmony offered, the Fuugle founders were excited. But they were tentative. Until, that is, they networked with some seasoned start-up friends they had made. As was pointed out, VCs rarely sign nondisclosure agreements (NDAs) anyway, and they can be quick to pass information along to people in their network for the purpose of vetting. What's stopping those people from using the information, or passing it along to yet another trust-level removed network? Zip, nada, nothing. That being the case, why not then actually control the information flow in a way that one can document who has looked at it, gain insightful analytics, and so on? The Fuugle founders immediately made the executive decision to launch from day 1 on the crowdfunding platform.

Using the gating features, the founders created some modest logic that allowed them to screen out contact from anyone except those people in at least their second-order social networks or who had high ratings associated with specified search tags. Ten minutes after pushing the Make Public button, another FundHarmony user noted Fuugle's public one-liner pitch and noted that the "search" tag needed a further and new qualification option of "ahead of time" and quickly added it. That elicited a visit from an *alpha tagger* user, the user with the biggest karma rating associated with the search tag, who then agreed with the new addition and helped cement the viability of the tag.

Subsequent users noticed this new "tagification" with intense curiosity, and they blasted out tweets and Facebook messages. Within hours, the blogosphere heated up (sort of a transient blogospheric global warming) with speculation about this most amazing new technology start-up. So much so that everyone wanted in as an investor, and Fuugle's funding commitment goal was met quickly. Fortunately for the flash-mob of investors, FundHarmony had thought ahead, and it had installed "circuit breakers" that allowed a cooling-off period before Fuugle could collect the funds. Almost no investors took the option to back out, and how right that decision turned out to be: Fuugle's eventual IPO was spectacular—but of course, its users already knew that it would be ahead of time.

Kicking It Downstream

Before fully dominating the crowdfunding space, the crowdfunding site FundHarmony was relegated to a particular part of the crowdfunding spectrum where it was focusing on early-phase deals. So at some point on the path toward Fuugle's quadrillion-dollar determination, Fuugle needed to transition to another site more fitting for later-stage deals. Fortunately, many of the crowdfunding platform providers had joined together previously in a coalition,[19] and they had decided that platform portability was important for situations like Fuugle's or in case regulatory shutdown forced projects to migrate elsewhere.

Fuugle benefited from the coalition's existence not just because it made it easy for Fuugle to move all the project files, social networking connections, and messages between platforms, but also because other larger funding-focused platforms actually bid for the deal. After diligently selecting one, the transfer was effected pending proper investor notifications, and Fuugle was on its way. To make this interoperability happen, all documents, activities, and social network diagrams were wrapped in standardized XML formats. And a new start-up-centric reporting format was created, in the spirit of what Extensible Business Reporting Language (XBRL)[20] is to public company reporting.

With the standardization across crowdfunding platforms came some new opportunities. Platforms could now negotiate cross-listing agreements, and they could acquire extra revenue sharing for the added exposure they offered. What was done for search advertising could now be similarly done on a crowdfunding site, only the "eyeballs" were more highly monetizable. This wasn't just a platform. It was an ecosystem of economic activity. Standardization became so much the norm that the crowdfunding industry decided to create its own exchange identifiers and assign "ticker symbols" to each project.

Intellectual Property Entanglements

Although crowdfunding had blossomed, it had some turbulent and trying times. In the industry's collective ebullience, not all crowdfunding sites had truly contemplated the ramifications of intellectual property ownership and transfer within a social networking setting. Some of the attraction and value that crowdfunding had tapped into were the participatory and emotionally attached investing aspects of it. But that meant, potentially, that founders and nonfounders were busily exchanging ideas, content, designs, and sometimes even software code. This was also true for the creative content part of the spectrum, whereby there was an exchange of script ideas and edits for movies, sound tracks for albums, and cover graphics for a fashion magazine. But in either case, this presented some real intellectual property entanglement issues, and it put crowdfunding on a collision course with patents and copyrights. Who owned all the ideas and content exchanged between parties on the crowdfunding site? And if a nonfounder presented an idea that was ultimately included in a patent application by the funded start-up, would that nonfounder facilitate the application process (the U.S. patent office legally requires that every inventor be listed on the patent)? In many ways, this was a problem shared with collaborative idea creation sites.

Fortunately, the issue was identified, and a fairly simplistic solution was presented by a group dedicated to the crowdfunding industry.[21] The creators of each new project would, before the project was surfaced to the public, choose how to compensate parties outside of their project based on the types and quantities of contributions. This was structured similar to a "call option" in financial terms, in the sense that if the project holders decided to incorporate or otherwise consume the content, they could call away the content from the producer of it in exchange for the compensation. On the funders' side, before they would be able to pledge any funds, they would contractually agree to the intellectual property option agreement. In a lot of cases, the compensation offered would be little to nothing. Perhaps contributors would get a signed album CD or DVD. Or the first bottle of next year's wine production. The important thing was that there would be a contractual agreement in place, before intellectual property entanglements could ensue—and that the integrity of the social contract would be retained.

The equity platforms were more sensitive to the issue, and they picked up on the solution early. That was quite insightful and fortuitous, as a number of music album and indie movie projects got hung up in litigation as soon as their sales volumes got interesting because the crowdfunding platforms did not enforce any such intellectual property discipline on the participants. Seeing the success, it was only human nature that small-time contributors felt that they deserved part of the financial rewards. In a very unexpected maneuver, the U.S. Copyright Office shut down two crowdfunding sites, until they cleaned up their acts. Since then, preexisting intellectual property agreements have become a crowdfunding industry standard. And a number of forward-thinking nations have decided to dispense with the patent system, after realizing it was imparting way more harm than good.

Chapter | 10

PREDICTION MARKETS AND MINING THE COLLECTIVE IQ

The short answer is that communities are better at both
identifying talented people and evaluating their output.
—Jeff Howe

I magine if intelligence could be broken down into a *spectral graph*, like the graphs you may have encountered in physics class, each bar representing the quantity of a particular band or component (for example, a frequency band) of the *spectrum*. For that matter, we could extend the spectral graph analogy to nearly any dimension such as personality, creativity, or diversity. Now let's say for sake of argument, that to solve a given problem, we know all of the components necessary to achieve a solution ahead of time. And therefore, we are able to create a representative spectral graph depicting the decomposition of the solution into its constituent parts and the magnitude of each part necessary.

This thought experiment lays down the framework for a very intuitive and simple way to understand why collective IQ works, and for that matter, why diversity is absolutely essential to any complex system. Let us now imagine that we incrementally add human resources (a.k.a. people) to a team that is working toward a goal of solving a complex problem set. And for each person involved, we also have a spectral analysis of his or her abilities, measuring the same components as does the graph of the problem under solution. As we add the second person, the collective IQ (the spectral graph representing the aggregate of all team members) grows. Some components (bands) of the graph now have bars where they were empty before, and some bars are a little higher, as the second person's talents in those areas are a little stronger. But note that the bars (measuring magnitude) for any given component do not necessarily increase in an additive fashion. Rather, they are more of a maximum function, equating to the highest magnitude across all the team members for any given component.

If the second person were to be very similar in talents to the first person, then the second person's impact on the aggregate spectral graph would be much less than if this new member were to have more varied talents. In fact, if we were to incrementally add a number of new members who were all similar in talents, then each new marginally added member would have less and less impact on the aggregate graph. Yet the complexity of the interactions (and management) of the team would increase significantly upon the addition of each new member. If the graph of the team at any one point matched the solution's graph, then the lack of adding new diversity would not be as problematic for that particular solution. But as is the case with solving many things worth doing, complexity is intrinsic. The mere fact that a solution is needed or desired implies that a "market" exists for the solution, whether the market is internal to a company or project or external in the sense that a solution is part of a product or service offered to someone else. And a market is a complex synthesis of many dynamically moving parts.

Continuing in our thought experiment, let's consider that after adding many team members, the team is only shy of aggregating enough collective IQ to match what was suggested by our solution graph, by a little extra magnitude of one component's bar, and it is completely empty in a couple of others. No matter how many new and similar team members are added, it is not as likely that the team will be able to achieve an ideal solution. The team's relevant collective IQ ceased to expand relative to the solution's requirements long ago. What was needed was not to add more "smart people" to the team; perhaps many of the team members were similarly smart. What was needed, instead, was the addition of more diverse members. Of course, in the hypothetical realm of this thought experiment, where we presupposed we knew all the needed elements of the collective IQ, a priori, the later team additions would have seemed almost comically misguided. We might have looked at the pool of available candidates and picked the ones that filled out our team's collective IQ graph such that it would meet the requirements of the problem's graph, in seeming disregard for their individual IQ qualifications.

In true life, the art of assembling a team suffers from further realities. One such reality is certainly that people individually (or in small groups) are not able to comprehend all of the facets of collective IQ that are required for solving any notable problem or performing any meaningful task. As a result, there are many "unknown unknowns," whereas we were able to presuppose them as "known unknowns." This is something addressed by various mechanisms applied to crowd dynamics, which we'll talk about. But a second and equally important reality is that very few people understand or truly respect collective IQ and the related construct of diversity. If they did, they wouldn't surround themselves with people much like themselves, at least not if they were trying to collectively achieve complex goals.

As an aside, consider the dimension of scores of many kinds of tests. An IQ test may yield a single number. A Graduate Management Admission Test (GMAT), a qualifying examination for entrance into a graduate-level business school, yields four scores, and one of them is for quantitative skills and another is for verbal capabilities. (For our purposes, we will ignore the two new test sections: integrated reasoning and analytical writing.) The verbal and quantitative scores can be viewed as spectral graphs of one or two bars. In science, such measurements would commonly be thought of as being so coarse grained and ambiguous as to be nearly useless. Just a thought.

Diversity Matters

At any rate, from the above discussion you may have had the intuition that an "outsider," someone who is much different in background or skills than the other team members, would be more likely than an "insider" to provide the catalytic final piece of the puzzle that would allow the team to go on to achieve the solution they need. This is true because the outsider would increase the team's chances of filling in missing pieces on the graph. If so, you'd be spot on. This intriguing phenomenon was well articulated in Jeff Howe's book *Crowdsourcing* in the insightful quote: "What's striking is that the best programmers aren't necessarily the ones making the most valuable contributions. The novices often provided a crucial tweak that led to a breakthrough."[1] Übergeeks, take note! Just as being a novice makes a person different enough to have those few catalytic components of diversity to drive breakthroughs, so does being competent in one field and attempting to solve problems in other disciplines—a point driven home by another observation from the same book: "We actually found the odds of a solver's success increased in fields in which they had no formal expertise."[2]

In problem solving, diversity matters, outside of the social motivations such as equality or reparation. It matters logically and statistically. But the importance of diversity is not limited to problem solving. Generating good ideas also tends to come from those people with more diverse inputs. Clay Shirky, in his book *Here Comes Everybody*, writes about a fascinating study from Ronald Burt of the University of Chicago called "The Social Origins of Good Ideas."[3] In the study, Burt was able to pin ideas generated within the company to those ideas that came from people with mostly ties (their network) *within a given department* and to those ideas that came from people with many ties *in other departments.* As it turned out, "the highest percentage of good ideas came from people whose contacts were outside their own department."[4] What's more, the bias toward good ideas was not at all from intellectual capacity. Rather, it was merely a result of exposure to preexisting ideas already residing in other groups! Or as Burt put it: "This is not creativity born of deep intellectual ability. It is creativity as an import-export business. An idea mundane in one group can be a valuable insight in another."

This is, in many ways, a similar observation to one made in *Crowdsourcing*: "A full 75 percent of successful solvers already knew the solution to the problem."[5] Wow, imagine what this could mean for big companies—they already have lots of solutions to their problems and harbor many good ideas that go unnoticed outside of their respective departments! This large group dilemma was also articulated in John Seely Brown and Paul Duguid's book *The Social Life of Information,* as expressed in the lament from a former Hewlett-Packard head: "If only HP knew what HP knows, think of how much more successful we would be."[6] And in fact, many large companies have recognized this dilemma, and they are now making efforts to know what they know. The mechanism of choice they are using is called a *decision market.*

A decision market is really another face of a prediction market. As of now, they are generally used internally within a company, as a way to apply the collective wisdom of the company to the act of decision making. This is, of course, a drastic departure from the classic decision-making process, which is based on the hierarchical and managerial org chart. Essentially decision markets allow a broad spectrum of participants (for example, employees at a company) to voice their opinions on various decisions (or add new issues to be decided upon), whereas the outcomes of the decisions are then generally factored into management's decisions. This allows the company to tap into inputs from the collective wisdom of the entire body of employees, rather than relying on the relatively narrow and often politically or selfishly filtered information flow up and down the corporate hierarchy.

While it might seem counterintuitive at first (at least to the extent that large companies generally don't quickly adopt anything new), there is an increasing adoption of the use of prediction markets across even the Fortune 500 companies. These companies suffer relatively the most when it comes to scaling issues related to the exchange of ideas and decision making, and especially when those issues are related to all other human-to-human complexities. So the companies have had little choice but to adopt new strategies to overcome issues related to such large scale.

If instead of asking "Should we do this?" people used the collective wisdom to answer "Will this happen?" but they used many of the same mechanisms, then they would have a *prediction market*. To a corporation or other group, in reality these two things are very closely linked if not the same thing. Prediction markets can be internally facing; Eli Lilly used an experimental market to test whether its employees would be able to predict the survival of drug candidates through the next round of clinical trials, which by the way, they did quite well at.[7] Or they can face the public. You may well have already heard of Intrade,[8] currently considered one of the leading prediction market platforms.

While in the general sense, prediction markets can take many forms, what has popularized many of the publicly facing modern-day versions is that they have cast predictions as financial instruments with prices based on the same mechanics of open market price discovery that also underlie other popular facilities such as equity markets. Real money is made and lost on contract positions on sites like Intrade.com, although users who prefer play-money prediction markets can use Intrade.net instead. There is seemingly no end to the number of outcomes one can take a position on. For example, there have been contracts for "Obama Administration— Repeal of the Don't Ask, Don't Tell policy" and "The Google Lunar X Prize to be won on or before December 31, 2012," and "The minimum Arctic ice extent for 2010 to be greater than that of 2009."

A few key ingredients make these kinds of collective wisdom marketplaces function, regardless of their form of output (for example, decisions or predictions) and of their exposure (for example, internal or public). Indisputably, the first is motivation. Financial motivations are obvious for commercial platforms such as Intrade, including pure-play upside investments as well as hedges on other financial activities. Unfortunately, there are also less obvious yet more nefariously financial motivations, like applying distortions to the price signaling mechanism of an instrument, which then tends to drive (potentially misguided) actions and decisions made by many other players based on the bogus price signaling—something innovative crowd mechanics could address.

Outside of financial, there are many other motivations driving participants to add value to the markets by way of their inputs. Some people are motivated by recognition of being good, and they like the bragging rights that come attached. But taking as an example an internal decision market at a nonprofit organization dedicated to eradicating hunger, there would be a complex myriad of inputs that must be considered when formulating an opinion on a decision regarding where to allocate resources next month. The motivations and considerations of such a decision, while complex, are not as important to understanding the efficacy of such a marketplace. In an environment replete with many decisions and predictions to be made, motivation serves as a resource allocator, notably that people will allocate their attention, time, and energy where it makes the most sense to them. That enhances the value of the market's outputs when, obviously, the participants' intentions are to create a better output in the spirit of the decision or prediction, but as important when participants who choose to add their inputs collectively have what economists call *local information*.

The economist and philosopher Friedrich Hayek, in his 1945 article "The Use of Knowledge in Society," encapsulated the essence of local information (which he then called "unique information") when he wrote: "Practically every individual has some advantage over all others because he possesses unique information of which beneficial use might be made, but of which use can be made only if the decisions depending on it are left to him or are made with his active cooperation."[9] This means that we all have our own version of "insider information."

The power of a decision or prediction market comes from the ability for the market to tease out the collective local information and express it as an outcome. And to the extent that motivation serves as a way of allocating and focusing the participants' limited resource budget (for example, time and energy) to add their local information inputs where it is believed they are the most relevant, impactful, and rewarding, then the accuracy and value of the market's outputs are greatly increased. Whether one zooms in to the level of synthesis behind decision making in a single person's mind or zooms out to the level of a large decision network, the processes are similar. But the level of local information is drastically different. The key is that the group of participants involved in a given decision or prediction have in aggregate the information (including local) needed to give informed inputs.

It's not necessarily the case that many of the participants who add their inputs to a decision or prediction market have high-quality or rich local information. In fact, it's not even necessary for a majority of them to be "right." If the market platform has a mechanism for discovering and assigning accuracy ratings for its participants, especially if those ratings are multifaceted in a way that allows ratings relevant to the desired outcome under question to be factored, then high-performance outcomes can yield from a platform that tolerates a great deal of noisy inputs, if not incompetence. This is because relatively stronger weighting can be applied to the inputs of participants identified as higher in performance. The power of the many can come from the few.

Now let's look at crowdfunding for a moment. In many ways, it already has or it has the potential to have all of the components of a prediction market! First, the fact that any given project receives funding from a substantial number of participants means that a reasonable sample size of inputs has coalesced around that project. That's no guarantee that the sample set represents a universe of quality local information. But it's a start. Second, the funding participants are generally self-selecting, which speaks to their motivations.

It's important to note that the measure of performance across various types of crowdfunding is far from homogeneous. In a creative project, success might be determined by a fan base funding a band album that when completed, pleases the fan base. In that spirit, the market properly identified and allocated capital to the project—it should be considered to be performing and accurate. That's something quite different in characteristic than a performance metric for predicting outcomes of equity-based start-up ventures. But it's still an outcome, and thus subject to prediction.

Much of this chapter's discussion thus far about prediction and decision markets has related to the inputs from the participants who essentially express a vote on a particular outcome. But crowdfunding offers something more profound. The listed projects themselves are a synthesis of local and macroinformation, potentially which have tapped into what one might think of as the "market of surplus problems and solutions."

As mentioned earlier in this chapter, when in search of a solution, it is important to realize that often it already exists—it's just not conveniently in the minds of the people in the immediate physical or virtual vicinity. As the catchphrase from the TV series *The X-Files* goes, "The truth is out there." And so are interesting solutions, although they traditionally have been hard to access. Now, with crowdfunding, the shadow market of surplus *problems* has just received some sunlight. That alone is a radical and step function kind of transformation to our world and to socioeconomics. And as an aside, according to Clay Shirky, author of *Here Comes Everybody*, we collectively have 1 trillion hours each year of "cognitive surplus" (free brain time).[10] So much time, and so many known problems and solutions to connect.

At end of the 1990s, a Toronto-based gold mining company called Goldcorp Inc. was facing flagging prospects as a result of strikes, debt, and high costs of production, and with gold prices hitting lows. Making matters worse, Goldcorp's geologists encountered difficulties evaluating mining potentials and locations. Rob McEwen became the CEO of Goldcorp not by way of having operational experience in the mineral extraction industry but instead by being a fund manager involved in a takeover. In 1999, McEwen was exposed to the open source phenomena of Linux, and he was intrigued by the efforts of distributed Linux developers who collectively created a world-class computer operating system.[11]

That exposure was the catalyst to an epiphany that McEwen had—and quite a radical one at that in the mining industry. In 2000, his company launched the "Goldcorp Challenge." The company released every bit of geological data it had for its 55,000-acre Red Lake property, and it offered total prizes of $575,000 for participants who came up with the best analysis methods and estimates. This was the open sourcing of data sets in what had always traditionally been an extremely secretive mining industry. Reportedly, more than a thousand outsiders participated. But they weren't constrained to geologists. There were many types of people attempting to solve the problems in many different ways: "We had applied math, advanced physics, intelligent systems, computer graphics, and organic solutions to inorganic problems. There were capabilities I had never seen before in the industry."[12]

The participants identified new sites, 50 percent of which were previously unidentified by the company. Even more incredibly: "Over 80 percent of the new targets yielded substantial quantities of gold. In fact, since the challenge was initiated, an astounding 8 million ounces of gold have been found. McEwen estimates the collaborative process shaved two to three years off the company's exploration time."[13] That was a story told in Don Tapscott and Anthony Williams's book *Wikinomics*. This story embodies the spirit of a famous quote from Bill Joy, cofounder of Sun Microsystems: "No matter who you are, most of the smart people work for someone else."[14] Perhaps the modernized version of that quote ought to be this: "No matter who you are, most of the important solutions are in the minds of people who work for someone else."

Sourcing the crowd is not merely a way to access surplus markets. *The crowd is the market!* All any one company can strive for is to have a tiny yet hopefully representative sample of the crowd. Therein lies a huge quandary for the traditional structure of businesses, and it is the basis for another major socioeconomic shift. What does *representative* mean in the new cross-discipline world? It's not just that the constructs of society and finance are subject to advancing complexity. The rate of change of innovation and problem solving are also marching forward according to their own Moore's law.[15]

If you've been paying attention at all to the start-up world, a proxy for the shape of the advancing wave of change, you may well have observed that creating new high-value propositions requires an increasing amount of cross-discipline thinking. But truly, this shift is occurring everywhere, in small and big companies alike. This is the cross-disciplinary century. Gone are the siloed days. One of the number of people recognizing this trend is Ram Charan, who in an article in *Fast Company* stated: "When multiple disciplines sit together, they see the total picture, isolate the major hurdles, and work together to solve the problems. The principle of working simultaneously is huge in making breakthroughs in innovation. Any handoff linearly is going to reduce your success."[16]

This has major implications that challenge the nature of how future companies will even be organized. If the future is interdisciplinary, fluid, and dynamic and it resists rigid structural boundaries, then can there be a hierarchy? Is the company organization chart anachronistic? What does a job title mean? Rather, the future of organizations is likely to be a collection of participants, with a very dynamic reshuffling or reassembling behavior, adapting continuously along with the organization's goals and current problem sets. And those organizational behaviors are very compatible with crowdsourcing and crowdfunding. The highly structured corporation is being upended, as is the role of an employee. Rather than being associated with rigid titles and job description boundaries, and for that matter only one company, tomorrow's employees may well be people who are fulfilling needs of a number of entities—they are part of a number of crowds at once.

The Performance-tocracy

That all may sound a little scary for "lifers" who have held long-term positions or worked at old-school companies. But it may actually be much more rewarding and provide a much better system for allocating labor, if properly implemented. After all, based on the thoughts of this chapter thus far, a functioning system would constantly inject intentional diversity (exposing people to situations and information that they were previously firewalled from) and be able to assess people's stronger traits algorithmically via their inputs into the decision and prediction markets (making for better placements than the HR department can achieve).

If the organization chart was the human-centric (and often political) platform for yesterday's organization, electronic platforms are enabling the rise of the performance-tocracy (which we like better than *meritocracy* because *performance* has the connotation of being measured), allocating people to tasks for which they are good at (or as was mentioned, for which they add diversity). This is a fantastic segue into some other powers of the future crowdfunding platform.

Think about the way in which start-up valuations have been negotiated in the past. In nearly all cases, there were really only a limited number of participants: the start-up in question and a set of potentially interested financiers. Ideal pricing occurs when a reasonably large set of participants finds a balance point at which they meet, that is, price discovery as in any open market. The problem in the traditional start-up valuation process is the limited set of participants. As a result, rather than achieving a true market price, what is really reached is a price (and deal terms) biased toward advantaging the side with the greater leverage.

Furthering this distortion is the potential in a very nontransparent (and kind of "small world") venture financing industry for price and terms collusion, or at least in the case of syndication, for one party really setting the price and the others following. None of this is very true to price discovery. But a crowdfunding platform can provide just that, by adding prediction and general market facilities to allow the crowd to drive valuations and predictions. Having a large user base with a diverse set of talents lets the platform tap into the pool of varied local information, assessing potential outcomes and valuations better than any limited set of players could ever achieve. Even without the extra sophistication of prediction markets, having a reasonably large number of funders automatically subjects the start-up to a more market-driven valuation. In fact, valuation as a discrete process goes out of vogue.

When considering the *rolling round* (or *rolling close*) phenomenon, whereby smaller and more incremental funding is acquired, the crowdfunding marketplace allows for a real-time, market-driven mechanism for automatically valuating pricing. Moreover, it allows for both price and deal terms to adjust based on when any given funder commits funding, which will facilitate better terms for earlier commitments. And as such, funding and secondary markets for early investors really should be part of a relatively seamless marketplace.

The start-up YouNoodle[17] was for some time focused on using prediction markets for assessing start-up valuations, but it seems to have, at least temporarily, switched its focus a bit to scoring the probability of success. The thing about prediction markets is that they require a reasonably sized set of people adding inputs for any one prediction, and that set is generally only a fraction of the total members on a particular service. A fairly popular crowdfunding platform would be a much better candidate, as it would already have a sizable universe of motivated and relevant parties.

Ultimately, a specialized prediction market facility that spans crowdfunding sites is an exciting proposition. That's another motivation for good APIs. It's still early in the game, but let's take the plunge and advance the prediction that traditional "market comps" and fuzzy math in start-up valuations will not survive this decade. In the same way that "the truth is out there," also "the price is out there," and it lives in the collective minds holding a complex of local and macroinformation.

One of the anticipated innovations (if we can get regulators to play along), much in the spirit of the "finders" meme, is for the people who are highly performing at evaluating funding pricing and terms (the earlier they are, the better) to be rewarded by various aspects of the platform. Perhaps they'll actually receive securities or perks from the project undergoing funding as a reward for their performance. Or perhaps they receive rewards from the platform or from special sponsorship, both of which were possibilities from the prediction market offering from Predictify, unfortunately no longer in operation.[18] Although prediction markets are best when more tightly coupled with crowdfunding platforms, the beginning of another generation of them is emerging—for example, Inkling,[19] which focuses on the more general idea of an evaluation and opinion poll market.

Price isn't the only thing worth predicting. Knowing which projects will achieve funding goals and which ones will subsequently achieve a successful business (or nonbusiness) outcome are also interesting. This knowledge can also be the province of various parties in the performance-tocracy who not only can potentially make a living by being right often and early, but can also enable many other ecosystems players who need to use such predictions as filters in what would otherwise be a daunting and noisy search universe.

What's an Expert?

As discussed previously, an interesting phenomena that is occurring is the diminishing durability of the "expert." This is, in part, a consequence of the increasing rate of change of social and technological forces. And it is, in part, a result of the shift toward the cross-disciplinary nature of our world. Expertise is now more transient than ever before, and today the moniker "expert" tends to evoke thoughts of someone who used to be good at something that has since changed. It's important that platforms recognize this and that they weight recent expertise ratings more heavily than past ratings. However, each area of expertise comes with its own rate of change, something that an intelligent platform (especially with good tagging) can recognize algorithmically. Or as a high school woodshop teacher used to say, "Let the machine do the work."

The landscape of change is far too complex to track manually. Rather than assessing people monolithically with an area of expertise, a performance-tocracy knows the levels of performance (and earliness) across a spectrum of fields and characteristics. Those levels ebb and flow. Using the spectral graph metaphor, our performance is best thought of as a many-components graph of ratings, defined by a snapshot in time. These kinds of multi-faceted assessments would be really useful for determining team diversity—something that, as was discussed, is essential going forward.

When talking with many people about prediction markets, the most common skepticism surrounds the dubiousness of a large pool of people making active inputs. As already discussed, most people are passive consumers, and so it's a very reasonable first-order thought. At least it is until one realizes that there really is almost no such thing as true passivity, other than sitting vegitatively in a dark cave, and that only counts if you don't have your smartphone with you such that it's not transmitting GPS coordinates. For just about all other activities, especially ones online, you are making *active* and *passive* decisions and predictions constantly; you just don't realize it.

Do you tend to look at funding opportunities tagged with "biotech"? Well then, you have now received an imputed "biotech" tag, and by the way, if you tend to read through the profiles of projects that have successful funding and, possibly, business outcomes, the platform knows that too. Now you've become a biotech expert, and your activities are factored as part of the prediction network for biotech plays. As is the case in much of human behavior, what you do is often far more important (and indicative) than what you say. Ask the dating sites if you have doubts. Passive activities in prediction markets are vastly important, and there are a lot of them on a crowdfunding platform—many more than on a vanilla prediction market platform. Active inputs will occur, as long as motivations (that is, incentives) are there. And motivations are necessary. But it's not necessary to have a large amount of active inputs to have an extremely valuable platform.

Trendspotting

Being involved early in successful projects will be extremely important to many crowdfunding ecosystem players, especially the professional ones. This is, of course, exacerbated by the shift in the offering of better terms to earlier investors (as it probably should have always been). Poaching off of more agile financiers by following them in a funding round used to be a viable strategy; now it's not enough, or at least a poacher's financial performance will not be as good. Spotting trends in real time is extremely helpful—knowing them ahead of time even more so. A crowdfunding platform is a rich ecosystem for trend analytics, not just for the projects being funded but for leading indicators of where major technological, economic, and social changes are headed. Adding prediction markets features pushes the envelope that much further.

Recently, there was a *TechCrunch* posting, purportedly of Ron Conway's confidential investment guide entitled "Tech Megatrends,"[20] which does a good job distilling a number of trends into a matrix, along with some relevant companies. For the most part, to those who are "dialed in," the list didn't have any big revelations. User comments in response to the post reflected this sentiment. A personal observation, and one that is quite a different point than the *TechCrunch* posting makes (and what actually makes this post newsworthy), is that this list is likely human generated.

With the rich ecosystem and infrastructure that crowdfunding can provide, this kind of list can be automatically generated in real time. Furthermore, it can be more extensive, accurate, and timely, and it can be personalized to any given participant. Essentially, the platform could generate custom "heat maps" for whatever fields of interest exist. That would be interesting enough. But with prediction markets, why not ask the market what trends *will be* hot soon? How about having next month's "heat map" delivered today? Now that's news! And there's no reason it can't or won't be done. Why? Because as the scholar Friedrich von Schiller once said, "In today already walks tomorrow." The seeds of tomorrow's events have already been planted in today, something that is comprehended in the collective of local knowledge. The synthesis of that knowledge is something well done by prediction markets. And that's what a crowdfunding platform is, or can be.

Speaking of performance, if you imagine that ecosystem players are also playing a role in the prediction markets, then they will also have trend-oriented performance ratings. Having a good score sheet in this area will be instrumental in getting a lot of deal flow, which of course will drive more players to interact with the prediction markets.

The Market Is the New Seniority

In a less volatile world of innovation, where technologies could last decades or longer, the concept of seniority made sense. As humans, we require the constant use of shortcuts, and perhaps seniority was as good a shortcut as any other possibilities for determining the capacity for handling responsibility of a given set of future tasks. If people had been doing something for a length of time, wouldn't that make them more likely to know how to do it, and more so than others? The problem with all of this is that seniority (and its cousin, experience), in its use as a valid shortcut, was predicated on low rate-of-change environments. But what we have today are increasingly higher rate-of-change trends, across the board, in social networking, technology, finance, and other areas. The same compression that has forced problem solving, and thus interesting solutions, to go multidisciplinary also has drastically outmoded the concept of seniority.

Past "experience" is especially dangerous in the hands of decision makers when that experience drives decisions that cross a time period when radical change has occurred within related fields. It's likely intuitive, but also simple to explain this. Selecting decision makers by way of their past experience equates to selecting a one-person prediction market, primed by historical data. For this to work out well, it's really important that the future look a lot like the past. But in environments of change, to survive well, that one-person prediction market would need to be much more of an arbitrator and synthesizer of a large number of inputs from a reasonably large number of people. Well, that's what a prediction market is, only it can scale much further. At any rate, since a lot of crowdfunding has served the indie movie and music categories so well, let's have a comical look at some apropos predictions made from "one-person prediction markets" of their times, from an insightful and entertaining book, *Inventing the Movies*:

> If we put out a screen machine, there will be a use for maybe about 10 of them in the whole United States. With that many screen machines, you could show the pictures to everyone in the country—and then it would be done. Let's not kill the goose that lays the golden egg. —Thomas Edison on movie projectors

> The public will never accept it. —Kodak founder George Eastman on movies with sound

> Sound is a passing fancy. It won't last. —MGM executive Irving Thalberg[21]

Making intelligent predictions or decisions (which are inherently founded on many predictions) involves an incredible amount of information and trend synthesis. Fewer and fewer situations allow for this synthesis to be done within a single mind. That is pushing the value of synthesis to the markets, be they decision, prediction, or otherwise. Meet the new form of seniority.

Prediction Markets Commoditized

Prediction markets have come to the masses, and they've also gone open source. Zocalo[22] is an open source toolkit (written primarily in Java) for building prediction markets, and it has been used for several research projects resulting in PhD and MS theses, as well as for technical papers. Another example, a more recent Drupal-based open source project, called Open Prediction Markets,[23] has a similar aim. Perhaps newer ones will arrive or be developed specifically for crowdfunding.

With new crowdfunding platforms comes access to a torrent of new information and crowdsourced vetting. As platforms mature, we will have a very good idea who excels at vetting particular start-ups, and thus a large-scale prediction market for vetting start-ups is born. And it will be far more sophisticated, and it will work at lightning speed. This opens up an enormous potential to bring Venture Capital into this century. Rather than relying on a small network of people, a platform used as a prediction market essentially takes inputs from the crowd and biases each based on the individual's performance. This has been applied with a high degree of accuracy in nearly every other field. And it will be applied to start-up financing as well.

Demonstrating the potential power when applied to start-ups is a blog post from yours truly.[24] Realizing that CrunchBase (an open source database of information relating to start-ups) in many ways presages what will be a treasure trove of start-up data available via crowdfunding, wouldn't it be interesting to see if applying some form of quantitative screen to the data set could affect performance?

Being in the start-up world for so many years had given me an intuition about something that could be used to predict start-up failure, sort of an ESP for the "dead pool." So I endeavored to apply the observation to data available on CrunchBase, given the limitations of that data. Quick analysis, although not officially "scientific," proved a lot of potential in that intuition.

The essential technique was to download the data set from CrunchBase and use the data only in divining the ability of the failure predictor to assess which start-ups would end up in the dead pool (the crowdsourced input to the synthetic prediction market). A completely different data set of start-up investment outcomes came from the Kauffman Foundation's Angel Investor Performance Project (AIPP),[25] the larger of a few such surveys. The data from the AIPP is complete enough that one can get a handle on angel returns by selecting random samples as portfolio scenarios and calculating associated returns. But with the correlation results of the failure predictor from CrunchBase in hand (using a logistical regression for the math types), the predictive advantage was then applied to the AIPP data, to simulate the returns of a prediction market–enhanced portfolio. The results: a random sample of the AIPP data had an internal rate of return (IRR) of 30 percent, while the enhanced method returned 46 percent! (See Figure 10.1.)

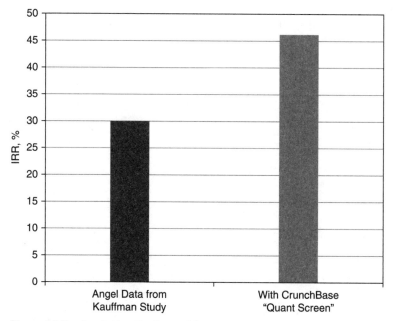

Figure 10.1   Predicting the Rate of Start-Up Failures

Sources: Ewing Marion Kauffman Foundation, *Angel Investor Performance Project* (AIPP), sites.kauffman.org/aipp, and AngelList, http://angel.co/jobs-act.

And that was just one of many improvements to come. Now certainly the CrunchBase data has a natural bias reflecting the dependency on the people who report it, as does the AIPP data—the point was more in showing the potential. But after writing that post, other people replied via e-mail, saying that they were researching their own "quant screens" and found similar gains.

Encouragingly, the early adopters of the venture funding community have recognized this predictive power of crowdfunding. The founders of AngelList, a widely popular site for entrepreneurs to connect to accredited investors, jumped into the fray during the time of congressional hearings related to crowdfunding, and they created a pro-crowdfunding petition.[26] Over 5,000 members from that community showed their support. And in the February 2012 issue of *Venture Capital Journal*, in an article about crowdfunding entitled "Funding Bill Stirs the Crowd," microfund VC Manu Kumar of K9 Ventures ushered in a new era of investment intellectualism, stating: "Having companies that have been proven out by using crowdfunding will only create better pickings for the venture capital industry to come in and scale those startups."[27]

Chapter | 11

THE INTERSECTION
WITH CROWDSOURCING

Chaos results when the world changes faster than people.
—Anonymous

Roughly speaking, one uses crowdsourcing to gather inputs from a crowd to get something *done* and crowdfunding to get something *financed*. But as is commonly the case, a considerable number of projects that need to be financed also need many other inputs to achieve their ultimate goal. And thus arises the interrelatedness and myriad hybrid model opportunities between the two, especially given a very shared set of group dynamic underpinnings. Even more significantly, to generally offer crowdfunding with only the ability to map financial inputs to the already manifold outputs (for example, tiers) is to monumentally starve the emotional and social attachments that are the binders and force multipliers in crowd behaviors to begin with. This would undoubtedly be even more pronounced for projects that offer only higher stakes, due to the lack of rewards to those who would otherwise add significant yet unaccounted-for value, and who would thus perceive (and rightfully so) relative unfairness.

No Network, No Funding

Unless some real outlier funders enter the equation with big increments of money, a project that doesn't elicit a following around its proposition doesn't usually get funded. While crowdfunding has shades of a popularity contest, it's generally a two-way street of value exchange in an open marketplace. And it's important to honor that exchange—especially because it's part of the social contract. Imagine for a moment, the following hypothetical. A documentary project team seeking capital via crowdfunding is only muddling along in terms of their progress on the funding front. There is only one week to go before the funding deadline they assigned, and they'll receive nothing if they can't push the total funding commitments to their funding goal.

Along comes 14-year-old Samantha, who randomly found out about the project to create a documentary on her favorite music artist. Samantha has little or no cash to crowdfund anything, but she carries something of far more value to the project: she has a massive circle of Facebook friends who also share her love of the same music genre. And she is a prolific user of Twitter. Wanting to help out, she blasts out messages on Facebook and Twitter about this cool new documentary, and within less than a day, the following around it and its associated funding go viral. The funding goals are met, due in large part, to the actions of one 14-year-old girl with no available monetary capital. The crowdfunding platform that was used only allowed the mapping between monetary inputs to an arbitrary set of rewards or returns. The documentary project team chose a typical "tiered" strategy, with increasingly larger sizes of investments parlayed into more premium rewards. For $25, one could receive a DVD when the documentary was finished. But for $2,500, the funder would get to invest in and make an appearance in the movie. Sadly, although Samantha arguably catalyzed funding, she received nothing in return. And it will be the last time she ever gives up so much value to "freeloaders," a sentiment that is shared by a number of many other participants in crowdfunding.

Very few crowdfunding sites or projects get this right. This crowdfunding sentiment could easily be called the *first timers' syndrome*. Until it's commonplace to properly reward all parties, the social contract is broken and a lot of ill sentiments can develop. To a first timer, the initial excitement of being part of something really cool and interesting is a big driver. But vis-à-vis other people in the collective, participating in what is perceived as a relatively unfair reward system, human nature drives a much more negative and visceral response. That's reason enough to prognosticate that in the future, most successful crowdfunding sites will offer mechanisms to map nonmonetary inputs into rewards.

Now imagine instead that the crowdfunding platform had options for offering rewards for a rich set of inputs from a project's fan base. The documentary project team decided to use a number of these options. For example, *per-person referral tags* were made available so that people in the fan base like Samantha could refer friends to the project's case on the crowdfunding site, and she would get credits for each allotment of people she referred. These referral credits would apply just as much as cash credits to receiving rewards.

The project team also needed to borrow some equipment, and thus they made a proposal to trade equipment usage for a number of documentary DVDs. And being on a shoestring budget, some help was also needed editing the film. In exchange, the film editor's name would be boldly displayed in the credits section, good for a résumé. In this alternate-world hypothetical, it would actually be possible for Samantha to be at or near the top of value contributors for the project. And who knows, she might even win an appearance in the documentary. That would cement her bond with crowdfunding, as it would materially align the rewards of crowdfunding with the values that the crowd delivers.

But there are many other reasons for the hybridization of crowdsourcing and crowdfunding. It's not just about perceived fairness (which, by the way, is a *major* issue in group dynamics or any open marketplace). It's also about involvement.

Crowdfunding Crowdsourced Ideas

It's easy to get wrapped up in the thinking that crowdfunding is only about people with ideas looking to get funded to implement those ideas. That's certainly an important part of crowdfunding, but the potential is much bigger. But as was discussed previously, there is actually a *surplus market of interesting problems and solutions* (that is, ideas). This phenomenon is also, to a degree, balanced by a number of very talented and motivated people who are in search of good ideas. Let's call this the *talent surplus*. Crowdfunding presents a forum, for the first time, to really connect these two surplus pools with huge scale.

One small but important tweak that can be applied to many crowdfunding platforms is to allow disassociation of ideas and projects. Many people tend to default to thinking about either as emanating from the same source. But to really make crowdfunding interesting and to enable the exchange of surpluses to flow, it's helpful to allow ideas to be posted, gain traction from the crowd, and then be picked up by talented people who are attracted to the idea and who will actually run with it. From that point forward, the project would have the same progression as any other project.

Ideas (even outside of officially proposed projects) are subject to applying all the same crowd dynamics, including gaining traction and prediction markets. In the spirit of the prior discussion about converting all types of contributions to the same reward systems, one could even envision an idea as the very first contribution to a project. In order to pick up the network of interested parties surrounding an idea with traction, perhaps a potential project holder would create a proposal to adopt the idea, including the terms of rewards to the idea's author in exchange. And perhaps another issue of which project to assign the idea and its fan base to is solved again by using the crowd. Perhaps the crowd around an idea should decide which project it gets attached to. The latent idea market is huge, and much of it lives in the minds of people who will never do anything with their ideas. That used to be an unfortunate condition, but perhaps the future will flip this equation around.

The Crowdfunding and Crowdsourcing Nexus

There are so many different crowdsourcing websites, and each has its own focus. This chapter is not so much about advocating for the reimplementation of their functionality as part of a larger crowdfunding platform as it is about conveying and stimulating thoughts of the power of their integration and partnership in a larger system. As the future of crowdfunding unfolds, it's pretty clear that both camps will enjoy synergies and a lot of opportunities for partnerships. Whether it's a need for logo design, proofreaders, language translation, software coding, a camera person, or studio time, many projects need help. Crowdfunding is force multiplied by crowdsourcing. The winning platforms will take advantage of that. As the business paradigm evolves, it will be hard to find a part of it that isn't affected in some way by the potential to reach out to the crowd. Money is the narrow band of light where crowdfunding really got its start. The entire spectrum is where it's headed.

Chapter | 12

THE NEW INVESTMENT MODELS

Once a new technology rolls over you, if you're not
part of the steamroller, you're part of the road.
—Stewart Brand, publisher of the *Whole Earth Catalog*

When contemplating the way forward and the potentials of crowdfunding, an easy trap to fall into is thinking about crowdfunding as a funding "alternative." In its current form, its relative youth might make it feel that way. Conversely, the entrenched system of funding imposed on us feels so mainstream. But to even frame the debate that way is to misunderstand the situation and, more specifically, to ask the wrong question. The relevant question is not about alternative versus mainstream. It's about natural versus unnatural.

Whenever any kind of construct is created that does not align in a reasonable and balanced way with the goals of the participants, it is distortive. When imposed on inefficient or captured markets, such imbalances can continue for long periods of time. They can even go on unnoticed or masked by other macrotrends. For example, in the late 1990s, the Venture Capital industry looked like it could not stop financing new start-ups or exiting previously funded ones, evoking the hyperbole "when pigs fly." But the truth is, Venture Capital has lived only to serve Venture Capital. And Hollywood has lived only to serve Hollywood. Neither has been generally aligned with its participants but rather, has dictated the terms of the relationship. That unnatural distortion couldn't last forever; natural forces have a way of ultimately winning. Gravity works, even on flying pigs, and now it's raining pigs.

Crowdfunding is a market of and for the participants. And when you look at the financing environment in that light, the real trend becomes much clearer. We are witnessing the system righting itself, returning to a natural marketplace. But this marketplace that is characterized by an exponentially complex network of participants and the resultant velocity of ideas that are exchanged is beyond the capacity for any incumbent financing industry to fathom, let alone manage or arbitrate. And so, the real questions moving forward relate to how existing (and new) forms of financing will cooperate with crowdfunding, not the other way around. This will be a decade of many hybridized financing models, with crowdfunding cooperation as part of their DNA.

Venture Capital Meets Crowd Capital

On July 6, 2010, Grow VC (a start-up seed capital crowdfunding website) announced something profound to crowdfunding's future: the "Virtual VC Co-Investment Fund,"[1] which enables Venture Capital to participate in Grow VC's seed investments. This was a milestone in the evolution of crowdfunding: the cooperation and hybridization of the old and the new financing models. *Conceptually*, the crowd became truly heterogeneous in terms of the sizes of potential per-investor contributions available to projects, the sizes of the aggregate "ask," and the professionalism of the participants (amateurs and professionals alike). With this signal of what's to come in crowdfunding came a very promising change in the nature of financing, especially for, but not limited to, early stage.

Thus far, crowdfunding has more or less been confined to funding projects that require relatively smallish funds, except for a few outliers that gather massive public exposure and funding. Unfortunately that precludes many powerful and economically interesting ideas that are capitally intensive in nature, such as those in material sciences, life sciences, electric vehicles, clean technology, and deep software infrastructure. But with the advent of hybridization and cooperation of financing models, along with the also newer rolling close trend, we can now look forward to a future when nearly anything and everything can be crowdfunded.

To the entrepreneur, a hybrid of VC and superangel and crowd participants offers a wider spectrum of financing options and ask sizes, while at the same time giving a lot more visibility. To the VC, using the crowd's affinity groups, prediction market capacity, price discovery, risk sharing, and huge reach is a win for the agile players. There are also a lot of opportunities for using the social networking aspects of crowdfunding platforms to identify the best ecosystem players to perform diligence, legal, accounting, and other important types of work.

As an aside, while it's rewarding for a trend forecaster to be materially ahead of the news, it was more than welcome to see Grow VC's Co-Investment Fund news. That same day, Part III of your author's presentation "The New Face of Venture Capital"[2] surfaced on *VentureBeat*[3] and predicted (as measured in hours) the coinvestment model.

Incubators and the Crowd

As discussed previously, incubators and other seed-stage capital formation devices have become quite popular and have been proliferating rapidly. But they come with their own issues. To holistically solve these deficiencies in the incubator funding model would necessarily involve networking them all together, given the lack of ability to tap the collective wisdom (and collective funding capacity) that underlies the deficiencies to begin with. So what would that look like? What if participants from one site could reach into the other sites to fund other projects, look to join other projects, and so on? The boundaries between incubators and crowdfunding would get really fuzzy, if not irrelevant.

As the real power of this model stems from the attachment to the greater crowd, it's perhaps more notionally accurate to think about an incubator persona or "brand" mapped onto a crowdfunding platform. For example, if a viable crowdfunding infrastructure had already existed including the ability to create a branding face, the Stanford Student Enterprises (SSE) Labs could have been launched with a few clicks of a mouse. In fact, this is our forecast of where the future of incubators lives. Whatever value that the incubators would otherwise offer in terms of start-up nurturing, advisement, and local networking would still be valuable. But the start-ups would not be "walled in" to the boundaries of the incubator, nor would general investors be "walled out."

Crowd Capital Meets Crowd Capital

Because there are a number of twists on the way projects can get crowdfunded, there are some really cool opportunities to service the entire funding life cycle by using different forms of crowd-funding. As an example, the site Cofundit[4] offers crowdfunding of nondilutive debt financing for small and medium-sized companies (currently only in Switzerland) that have proven revenue streams.

While that wouldn't be the place to start a seed-stage company, it might be an excellent platform on which to seek a future round of financing after using a different platform to get started. There are many such permutations like this, and of course the funding experience gets better for entrepreneurs, as the ability to cross sites or have the various services cross-list increases. More is discussed on that, herein. But specifically, to facilitate this, it helps if the crowdfunding platform infrastructure and deal terms anticipate this.

Donations First, Investments Later

Another and pragmatic (in the sense that it's doable using what exists today) hybrid funding model is the use of a donation-based crowdfunding platform to get the initial funding, using a more emotionally attached fan base crowd who really wants to see the project happen. After using the funding to advance the project to the point of some form of market traction, or at least demonstration of market value, then subsequent rounds can be solicited with a more financial ROI bent. One could think of this strategy as a two-stage rocket approach. If the seed funding requirements can be met by crowdfunding, this has a number of advantages to the entrepreneurs, including preventing equity dilution and enabling the utilization of facilities that are fairly widely available. There are possibilities here, to offer special rewards to contributors in the first phase.

Here Comes Wall Street

As the seed-stage funding market has acquired newfound traction by way of the proliferation of crowdfunding and secondary markets, it's only a matter of time before the same minds that successfully applied complex mathematical models to other asset classes will take notice of the early-phase start-up market. Investing in risky start-ups used to be the nearly exclusive province of the venture finance community. And many in that community would argue (and a number have) that this exclusivity was due to special talents and knowledge within that community. But the collective IQ is always much higher than any group's sample, especially for smaller groups.

The reality is that the early-phase start-up investment field has historically been very opaque. But with increasingly transparent seed-stage mechanisms that tend to also be inherently computer accessible, the door is now opening for access by the rest of world, not just by private investments from unsophisticated investors. Rather, going forward, there is a huge opportunity for VC's "big brother," Private Equity, to play in the start-up sandbox. Keep in mind that these are the players who hired many top mathematically minded PhD types and pioneered the worlds of black-box investment and prediction markets. And there will be a huge amount of data available, given that the crowdfunding platforms are willing to provide it.

What's even more exciting is that there is a whole new "greenfield" out there, relating to how the public markets can gain access to start-ups as an asset class! Imagine for a moment an investment vehicle that is public "on top" (that is, it is a publicly traded instrument) and private "on bottom" (that is, it invests in private start-ups). Let's say that this investment vehicle is managed by an investment firm of sorts, which has the charter of investing exclusively in crowdfunded start-ups in the nanotechnology field. How this investment firm makes its capital allocation decisions is subject to another host of potentials. Decisions could stem from prediction markets, classic human-oriented investment thinking, or even a democratic vote from the shareholders.

In any case, the promise of this new style of investment vehicle is that it opens up investments in start-ups to the general public. In the way that people can trade stocks in their investment

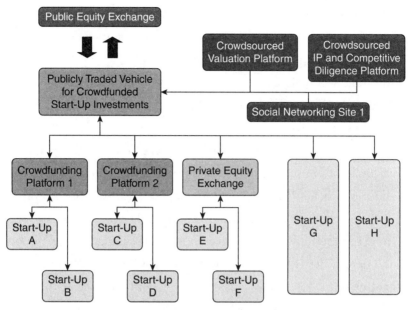

Figure 12.1   How Public Markets Can Gain Access to Start-Ups as an Asset Class

Source: Kevin Lawton, "The New Face of Venture Capital: Crowdfunding's Big Bang," *VentureBeat*, July 6, 2010, http://venturebeat.com/2010/07/06/ the-new-face-of-venture-capital-crowdfundings-big-bang/.

accounts, they could buy exposure to the future of nanotechnology, much like buying an exchange-traded fund (ETF).[5] But this wouldn't be limited to individuals. Many other participants would have access: mutual funds, pension funds, sovereign wealth funds, hedge funds, and so on. This was the vision that elicited the name of Part III of "The New Face of Venture Capital" series written by your author, entitled "The Big Bang of Crowdfunding,"[6] which included the following illustrative depiction (Figure 12.1).

Have you ever checked out the investment service kaChing (now known by the much classier name Wealthfront)?[7] It was a new way to find investment managers to manage your portfolio and to track their performance in a far more transparent way than ever before. The coolest and most radical facet of kaChing was that after you selected a suitable investment manager, you could have your investment account autotrack that manager's decisions. Managers who performed well and attracted a good following could potentially do quite well because their investment decisions would scale to an arbitrarily sized following (as would the commissions they received).

Now imagine a popular equity-focused crowdfunding platform that has a lot of users who have don't have as much time and inclination to allocate the few thousand dollars they have on account. But they realize that there are some top-gun investors on the site who are incredibly good at investing in particular areas of interest. Therein lies the opportunity for the kaChing of crowdfunded start-ups—and for a new class of investment managers, the new "VCs of crowdfunding." In the way that people can import their investment history into kaChing, it may well become important to import one's credibility of picks on crowdfunding platforms. To the platforms out there, please at least enable this feature at a fun level so a history can be established. And for the hopeful managers of the future, get busy making picks!

As the funding paradigm shifts from being based on discrete rounds of funding to being based more often on continuous, rolling close funding, tomorrow's highest-performing investors (and investment managers) won't need to be only right. They'll need to be right *and* early. This is because start-ups may well (and probably should) elect to give better terms to the early investors. And *early* could mean days, hours, or even minutes. One could still tailgate, and there's no doubt the sheep will follow, but we're going to find out who's *really* good in this new age of financing start-ups. Asymmetric ROI will result based on "early-ness" (an almost Stephen Colbert[8] style term). Measuring this facet will not only be good for the résumés of high-performance investors, but it will also be good for seeding prediction market algorithms that drive further platform values.

A New Capital Allocation Mechanism

At its core, crowdfunding is a new (or at least reborn) form of capital allocation mechanism, whereby the capital tends to be allocated according to the collective will of the participants. Depending on the slant of any given project undergoing funding, or of an entire crowdfunding site altogether, *performance* as we may customarily think of the word may not be a fair or even relevant assessment. Rather, success in crowdfunding *some kinds* of projects is achieved when the projects that receive funding are a true expression of the crowd's collective will to allocate resources—and nothing else. This is especially true in rewards-based crowdfunding, but undertones of this ring throughout the whole spectrum.

When observing the significance of crowdfunding in this light, another potent realization becomes more apparent: the crowdfunding mechanism is an extremely natural fit for the capital and other resource allocation for projects of any sized community, be it a small neighborhood or an entire country. Rather than be filtered by the inevitable biases (and worse, corruption) of various intermediary committees, panels, and other bureaucratic forms, resources will be allocated according to the expression of the collective will, in the democratic spirit in which many modern societies were founded. And hopefully, these allocations will be steered or guided by forms of curation based on performance and community respect.

While researching crowdfunding, one very intriguing factor surfaced, one that many have confirmed. Crowdfunding is the one mechanism for which people of all political parties seem to come together on (except for perhaps those individuals who have a vested interest otherwise). Crowdfunding is without a political party. It draws its maximum power when the collective diversity is the greatest. And yet, it suffers no indecision. It will not produce utopia. There isn't a sense of wrong or right, only collective will. That opens some really interesting and culturally important new avenues.

At the Community Level

Imagine a hypothetical community that has a given pool of capital to be allocated to various public transportation–oriented projects. Rather than subject the capital allocation process to the cacophony of public voices, intense lobbying from a variety of businesses and organizations, and town hall meetings, the community members decide to use something much more modern. They create a crowdfunding compartment on a large website dedicated to the community, and they transfer the available funds into a newly created and associated account. Each of 10 possible projects is entered into the system, and each project has a minimum funding requirement. Among the 10 projects are community bikeway improvements, expansion of a community parking lot, and additional space for a weekly farmers' market. Each person who can prove residency is given an account, which can be accessed at home or at any public access point such as the public library. Or the account can be accessed from mobile phones via texting or the special mobile application provided by the crowdfunding company.

If this community is progressive, they may well overfund the bikeway and farmers' market projects but not fund the parking expansion plans. But if parking is a big issue, then it will likely get funded instead. This is the crowd speaking. They do not necessarily need to decide on exactly how the community bikeways will get expanded, although they can—project implementations can still be largely managed by teams of qualified people with the bigger picture in mind. But the choice of where to allocate capital will be the result of the collective will. And more to the point, it will be the result of democracy.

Stepping back for a moment, one might wonder why this isn't common already. Certainly before the advent of the Internet, and more recently until parts of the world and our culture became much more Internet accessible, this would have been difficult to implement. But it's a lot more doable today, and probably a lot more capital efficient.

Grants and the Arts

Open Genius is an Italian-language site that facilitates crowdfunding for research projects.[9] The crowd of scientists, enterprises, and other individuals qualifies the projects via peer review, and they decide which projects get funded. This is currently a donation-based service. But imagine what would happen to innovation in the sciences if instead of filtering government grants (which of course are generally sourced from taxpayer money) through a bureaucratic process, money were allocated to a pool using a model much like Open Genius. Not only would it allow the collective wisdom of the crowds to allocate capital, but also would allow the prediction market mechanics of expertise to more highly focus the allocation. And the peer review process would be opened to the same powerful dynamics.

It would be quite interesting to see governments, even in a "trial balloon" sort of way, utilize this newly available model. A very similar argument could be made for allocating capital for the arts. If anything, the strongest argument can be made for disintermediating any form of bureaucracy from interposing in the allocation of resources to the arts. And indeed, as mentioned in Chapter 5, Kickstarter announced in February 2012 that it was on track to provide more funding for the arts than the National Endowment for the Arts (an independent agency of the U.S. federal government). A question relative to the times is, why does any taxpayer money for arts or science get funneled through government bureaucracies?

Reinvigorating the Community

Robert Putnam's book *Bowling Alone* is a phenomenal look at the increasing disconnectedness that has occurred in society, stemming from the myriad changes in our lives, including television, computers, and suburbia. [10] Ironically, many of the things that make it easier to connect and to communicate have contributed to a sense of the lack of physical connectedness. But there's nothing saying it has to be that way. Cultures can "civicly reinvent" themselves, as the author Putnam states.

What if community crowdfunding were this century's "town hall"? But rather than the coarse-grained gathering mechanism of the past, it provided a new sense of attachment in the community issues and direction, and it provided a fine-grained way for parties with similar concerns and interests to coalesce. And not just coalesce in the virtual sense but meet face-to-face. Wouldn't people be more apt to focus their time and energy talking about the things that are relevant to them, and with the people who are most relevant, instead of attending more monolithic and large-scale town hall meetings? While there seem to be enough other reasons to try out community crowdfunding, this one is especially encouraging. An integrated crowdfunding community model could mean a form of social networking that reconnects people to their physical community.

The Virtual Tech Hub

Like many web technologies, it's quite possible to put a face on or otherwise overlay a persona or branding experience onto an underlying crowdfunding platform (a *white boxing strategy*). That being the case, then it's quite conceivable to easily build *virtual tech hubs*. While one could take that idea in a lot of directions, a very exciting application is in community empowerment. For example, imagine in a very point-and-click manner, creating a virtual tech hub for a particular poor region in Africa, on the infrastructure of an existing crowdfunding platform. Consider that funding could come from anywhere, but the projects have to be local with whatever geographic granularity is desired (even down to a village).

Obviously, there are many regulatory and legal issues to contend with, but the idea is to utilize existing crowdfunding infrastructure to lessen the burden of creating local innovation financing ecologies, including using local physical service providers as part of the crowdfunding network. These are the kind of world changing opportunities that lie ahead, and we have scarcely begun to explore them. So far, platforms such as Kiva have really provided only debt finance. But there are other forms of finance that can be offered (and are arguably better than debt), and many other services that integrated into the platform would provide a richer set of opportunities to put communities on the path towards self-empowerment.

Chapter | 13

REGULATION AND POLICY STATUS

Avoidance and force only raise the level of conflict. . . . They have become parts of the problem rather than the solution.
—J. Dececco and A. Richards[1]

The Current State of Affairs

"I think we're at the stage right now with crowdfunding that we were with eBay before eBay existed. When eBay started, the standard knock was that it was going to be an invitation to fraud. But eBay figured this out; they figured out a way to develop trusted networks so you wouldn't give your money to crooks,"[2] said Robert Litan, vice president for research and policy at the Kauffman Foundation. That well encapsulates the phase that crowdfunding has entered. Had eBay not figured it out, it would have perished, as people wouldn't have used it for long. Or had heavy new bureaucracy been established to regulate the space to "protect consumers," the model would have suffocated. Yet somehow, eBay fraud just doesn't make the headlines, now does it? Interestingly, a number of campaigns that had even a whiff of fraud were discovered early by the crowd and canceled quickly.

If we lived in a germ-free bubble, our immune systems would collapse. If there were never any fraudsters, we would have no immunity to fraud—no abilities to spot it, no credibility networks, no reporting mechanisms, no diligence companies, and no fraud education. We would all be pretty much dependent on a thick ineffective bureaucracy to "protect us." Unfortunately this has been the case, and for about 80 years, billions of people have fallen victim to this "bubble boy" investment syndrome. So much so that the regulatory complex created a name for the affected: *nonaccredited investors.* Had we gotten the investment regulatory bureaucracy out of the way many years ago, an entire ecosystem would have already existed that would have enabled individuals to deal with fraud. But a hyperventilating establishment—the same people who presided over a quadrillion dollars of notional global derivatives (known to common folks as *counterfeiting*) and a banking scandal of epic proportions (perhaps the jails are too full to accommodate bankers?)—just can't wait to interpose themselves in our lives and "protect us."

Leading up to the historic Jumpstart Our Business Startups (JOBS) Act signing in the United States, a "six pack" of bills that included provisions to legalize securities-based crowdfunding, the media was awash with pieces from both pro and con camps. If anyone is looking for an interesting sociology thesis, here's a big fat juicy one. Analyze a batch from either camp, choosing ones from authors who seem otherwise credible. Then correlate their conclusions, for or against crowdfunding of securities, by their knowledge levels of crowdfunding and social networking dynamics. Also assess and correlate to their conclusions their level of being in the "financial establishment." You probably know where this is heading.

By and large, people who wrote hit pieces had little clue about crowdfunding or social networking, and they often worked within

the establishment. The least qualified people wrote the most negative articles. These are many of the same people who wheel out the
"it's for your protection" speech. No protection needed for them
though; they're exempt. One such individual even wrote a lengthy
"peer-reviewed" paper that concluded that many people would lose
all of their money to fraud. Not once in the paper was either the
terms "portfolio" or "diversification" mentioned. Might one wonder
how investors could lose all of their money on a single investment
unless they roll the dice on their entire nest egg?

Perhaps the peer review process missed this reality. In a query
directly to the paper's author—surely they'd be delighted to hear
some constructive criticism—the author responded, "We'll just have
to agree to disagree." Agree on what, algebra? Putting 10 percent
in a fraudulent investment makes the net worth go to . . . 90 percent. Only in the highly regulated securities world, where exists
the reality distortion fields of massive leverage and derivatives, can
a 10 percent investment put the investor into bankruptcy. But never
let the facts get in the way of a good story (or hit piece).

In fact, an even easier way to see what a sham this "protection"
has been is to look at the risk versus reward of both penny stocks
(which of course are tradable by the public without any of the limits currently proposed for the crowdfunding exemption) and angel
investments. In a *Huffington Post* article entitled "Crowdfunding's
Fraud Bogeyman,"[3] written by your fearless author, the telling
graphic, reproduced here as Figure 13.1, explained the economic
suppression that much of the world has endured along with the
farce that is the mandate for banning general solicitation. The
more curvy line labeled "Angel" represents the profile of angel-
stage investments, from the Kauffman Foundation's *Angel Investor
Performance Project* (AIPP) survey. The X axis is ranked by deciles,
meaning, for example, that at the third decile, 30 percent of the
data is to the left on the graph. Only first-stage investments that
didn't take follow-up money were used because that made things

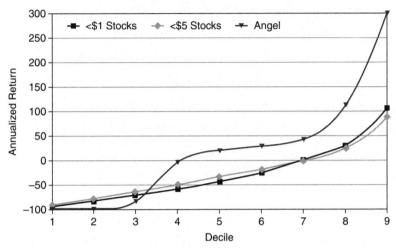

Figure 13.1 Annualized Returns: Early-Stage Venture Investments Versus Penny Stocks, November 2010–November 2011

Source: The line labeled "Angel" represents the profile of angel-stage investments from the Kauffman Foundation's *Angel Investor Performance Project* (AIPP) survey, July 2010. For the penny stocks (the other two similar lines), data was gathered for both sub-$1 and sub-$5 equities over the last year, from portfolio123.com.

easier and represents many small businesses that need money only to get off the ground. For the penny stocks (the other two similar lines), data was gathered for both sub-$1 and sub-$5 equities over the last year, from portfolio123.com. All are encouraged to further study a wider range of years.

What's astounding here is that, except for the worst third of either asset class (in which case, neither asset class did well), start-ups were less risky and had better returns than penny stocks, even though penny stocks are available to the general public without limit restrictions (but of course, there's a broker-dealer in there skimming transaction fees). Hopefully it's easy to see that in either case, one needs a diversified portfolio to mitigate risk—one really needs a diversified portfolio with the penny stocks since 70 percent of them lost at least some value. Now, if loss of investment money is so devastating, then why are we not hearing about it constantly? And why did we miss out on 80 years of enormous potential economic growth from funding small businesses, while we instead redirected money out of our local communities into large public companies?

Or better yet, *how much* did we miss out on? While that would be quite difficult to assess fully, we can assemble a few pieces of the puzzle that help provide a solid intuitive answer. The Kauffman Foundation released a report in its Research Series called *Firm Formation and Economic Growth: The Importance of Startups in Job Creation and Job Destruction.*[4] The graph in the report, shown here as Figure 13.2, provides one important piece of the puzzle: start-ups create most of our new jobs, something that Obama stated clearly in his speech at the JOBS Act signing. A second puzzle piece, perhaps of even more import, is an understanding of the suppression of the local economic multiplier effect

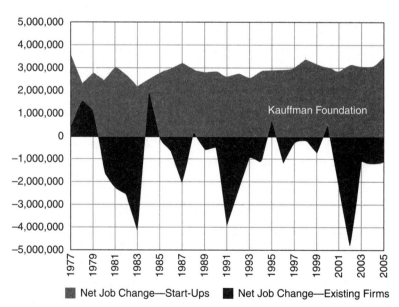

Figure 13.2 Start-Ups Create Most New Net Jobs in the United States

Source: Tim Kane, Business Dynamics Statistics, as cited in the Kauffman Foundation Research Series, *Firm Formation and Economic Growth: The Importance of Startups in Job Creation and Job Destruction*, July 2010.

that comes from well-functioning small businesses. Amy Cortese's book *Locavesting* explains that local businesses have a strong multiplier, say, of 3 to 10 in magnitude.[5] That means that for every dollar into a given business, that many more dollars of local economic activity are created.

For those who would like to deep dive into the economics of locality, the work of Michael Shuman is also highly recommended; he's one of the world's leading experts on community economics, a prolific author, attorney, entrepreneur, and cofounder of the Business Alliance for Local Living Economies (BALLE). His recent book *Local Dollars, Local Sense: How to Move Your Money from Wall Street to Main Street and Achieve Real Prosperity*[6] and his previous book *The Small Mart Revolution: How Local Businesses Are Beating the Global Competition*[7] are great places to start.

What is clear is that large transnational businesses often have multipliers less than 1. They actually suck money out of local communities, and they dump the money into foreign lands for production and tax sheltering. Of course, many of the early-stage investments that crowdfunding serves have a strong locality factor. And thus, the SEC suppresses $100 of investment money to stave off $1 of fraud from the bogeyman. More important, the SEC suppresses $300 to $1,000 of economic activity because of the local economic multiplier effect. And unfortunately, Wall Street has been most people's primary avenue for investment. "No" is not a risk mitigation strategy—it's a form of economic genocide, especially when the dictated "yes" option is an economic black hole.

In the *Bogeyman* blog post, the following challenge was made:

> Inherent in a fraudster's ability to steal all of our money via crowdfunding is for people to invest all of their money in one business. And yet, I cannot find a single person who thinks that doing so is a good idea. **If you find such a mythical person, please have him or her write a blog post about it, and forward me a link!**

This challenge has, at the time of writing, gone unanswered. The issue has always been about *failure*, not the bogeyman of fraud. Failure is mitigated by diversification, an education thing. It has nothing to do with regulation. And education is just the kind of thing best promulgated by industry organizations, not governments.

So it was very heartening and exciting to see the crowdfunding community go into full-throttle, proactive mode and get a jump on industrywide self-regulation, long before the SEC (which was given nine months, after the signing of the JOBS Act, for unelected officials to create yet another pile of fiat law, otherwise known as regulation) waves its magic wand and subsequently "protects us" with some kind of giant regulatory prophylactic bubble.

In the build-up before the JOBS Act signing, but when the prospects for the passage of any semblance of securities crowdfunding looked the least bit promising, the buzz from the crowdfunding camp went ballistic. Many platforms in the waiting surfaced their intent. Quite a few others are still lying in stealth mode. Likely many new designs on the space will come about. But the JOBS Act was an American crowdfunding phenomenon only in the way that landing a person on the moon was—the craft might have been American, but the entire world was watching. This is a phenomenon catching on everywhere. Fear is changing to urgency, as reflected in a pre-JOBS Act article entitled "Legalize Crowdfunding or Risk Losing Startups to U.S., CATA Says,"[8] conveying a warning signal from the Canadian Advanced Technology Alliance. That sentiment rings true in many places. And note to the rest of the world: behind the scenes, some countries are building their own rockets.

Which then raises an interesting question, "What about the existing platforms that were founded on the perks and donations model?" Thus far, it seems many of them have designs on adding in the option for equities and other securities-based projects, while perhaps not shaking up the existing tenor of the sites too radically.

Popular platform Indiegogo is openly examining the possibilities according to its CEO Slava Rubin,[9] for example.

A notable exception, though, is the platform that became to crowdfunding what Kleenex became to facial tissues—Kickstarter. Apparently they've drawn a line, and equity is on the *other* side. On May 22, 2012, well after the JOBS Act signing, Kickstarter cofounder Perry Chen made this statement: "We're not gearing up for the equity wave if it comes. The real disruption is doing it without equity. The real disruption is when you break down the funding of a project into all these little bits."[10] Considering Kickstarter has admitted it has taken VC money (possibly over $10 million of it[11]), this decision, for better or worse, will be debated for some time to come.

United States

The United States was the first country to create a law giving entrepreneurs and the general public the ability to participate in true crowdfunding, including those soliciting funding in exchange for securities (for example, equity, debt, or profit sharing). The JOBS (standing for the aptly named Jumpstart Our Business Startups) Act was signed into law on April 5, 2012.[12] The crowdfunding component of the act specifies the conditions under which entrepreneurs are allowed to "generally solicit," essentially meaning to tell the general public about an offer to fund the enterprise. Until the SEC regulation was created in the Securities Exchange Acts of 1933[13] and 1934,[14] these activities were covered by the First Amendment in the Bill of Rights:

> Congress shall make no law respecting an establishment of religion, or prohibiting the free exercise thereof; *or abridging the freedom of speech*, or of the press; or the right of the people peaceably to assemble, and to petition the Government for a redress of grievances [emphasis ours].[15]

The founding documents of the United States were constructed by founders who were quite justified in their significant paranoia about bad government (having had a brilliant case study of it already), but in later years the government went ahead and created the SEC. And that was the beginning of a nearly 80-year run of suppression of entrepreneurial free speech—and its descent into the corporatocracy that America has become, one that the founders so vehemently warned against. The JOBS Act is just the *beginning* of a reversal.

An excellent plain-English summary of the conditions under which the new crowdfunding provisions can be used was written by Shane Fleenor of the Funding Launchpad in an article entitled "An Authoritative Look at the New Crowdfunding Legislation."[16] The general requirements, as excerpted verbatim from his article with permission, are these:

A. no more than $1,000,000 is raised via crowdfunding in any 12 month period; and

B. no single investor invests more than a specified amount in the offering, namely:

   i. the greater of $2,000 or 5% of the annual income or net worth of the investor, as applicable, if the investor has annual income or net worth of less than $100,000; or

   ii. 10% of the annual income or net worth of the investor, as applicable, if either the annual income or net worth of the investor is equal to more than $100,000, capped at a max of $100,000 invested.

C. the offering is conducted through a registered broker or "funding portal" (a new term made up by the JOBS Act); and

D. the issuer complies with certain other requirements that we'll get to below [in the article itself].

There are also a number of further requirements and limitations on the crowdfunding platforms or intermediaries (the "funding portals," as they're called in the act), which are equally important to know about (excerpted from the same source):

A. providing certain disclosures and investor education materials to investors

B. ensuring that the investor has reviewed educational materials and answers questions indicating that he/she understands the risks involved

C. performing certain background checks on the issuer

D. provide a 21 day review period before any crowdfund securities are sold

E. ensure that an issuer does not receive investment funds until its target investment minimum has been reached, and that investors may cancel their commitments to invest as provided by the SEC (no word yet on how these cancellation provisions are going to look)

F. ensure that no investor surpasses the investment limits set forth above in a given 12 month period in the aggregate – i.e. the limits described above with respect to investors apply to all crowdfunding investments in a given 12 month period, not just to individual investments, and the burden is on the intermediary to monitor this

G. take steps to protect the privacy of investors

H. not pay finders' fees to promoters or lead generators with respect to investors (it appears to be okay to pay finders' fees for issuer leads)

I. not allow the intermediary's directors, officers or partners to have a financial interest in an issuer using its services

But then there are the future-tense SEC additions, based on language that states: "meet such other requirements as the Commission may, by rule, prescribe." In other words, unelected people currently on the SEC side of a revolving door with big banks can layer on more onerous rules, making crowdfunding as practically impossible as they see fit. Or as the article in *Bloomberg Businessweek* described, "The agency has until early next year to write rules governing who can buy and sell the stock and to establish safeguards against fraud—basically, erect a whole new regulatory bureaucracy."[17] This, of course, at least for those who have actually read the Constitution and Bill of Rights, is in violation of the Tenth Amendment:

> The powers not delegated to the United States by the Constitution, nor prohibited by it to the States, are reserved to the States respectively, or to the people.[18]

That passage simply states that if you're not representing the people (that is, you haven't been elected), you're not making law. Unfortunately, there's more to the story, and the requirements continue on to the "issuer," which is the entrepreneur who is issuing the stock or other securities:

A. name, legal status, address, website, etc.

B. names of directors, officers, and 20% stockholders

C. "a description of the business of the issuer and the anticipated business plan of the issuer"—the devil is really in the details of this one, and it remains to be seen whether the SEC will require this "description" to be 4 pages or 40 in order to be sufficient

D. prior year tax returns, plus financials—see below for details

E. description of intended use of proceeds

F. target offering amount, deadline, and regular progress updates through the life of the offering

G. share price and methodology for determining the price

H. a description of the ownership and capital structure of the issuer, including a lot of detail about the terms of the securities being sold, the terms of any other outstanding securities of the company, a summary of the differences between them, a host of disclosures about how the rights of shareholders can be limited, diluted or negatively impacted, "examples of methods for how such securities may be valued by the issuer in the future, including during subsequent corporate actions," and a disclosure of various risks to investors

Now, a few of these at least seem reasonable on the surface. But in (C) the anticipated business plan vagaries leave the door open for a lot of interpretation (and most early-stage technology companies don't make business plans anymore). The (D) prior year tax return requirement should be interesting, given that many early-phase companies that would want to use crowdfunding don't yet exist. Perhaps for requirement (G), the SEC will accept "share price determined by the market . . . like, duh!"

For those concerned with the regulatory details, reading a similar review after the SEC issues its associated fiat law is essential. But it's important to note that even after that time, the regulatory complex imposed on crowdfunding platforms could cause further delays, as they are forced to work through the red tape of becoming approved. If that weren't bad enough, have a look at the excellent document prepared by crowdfunding site RocketHub,[19] in the public comments area related to the JOBS Act.[20] It's an on-point analysis and critique of the crowdfunding components of the act, and points out a host of issues of ambiguity, vagueness, and relevancy.

Other major oversights were identified by Jenny Kassan[21] from Cutting Edge Capital: "There are a couple of things the law didn't address that I wish it would. One is a mutual fund for local business."[22] Kassan points out that it's extremely onerous to set up a fund for small local business. Taking her point even further, imagine if people could invest parts of their retirement vehicles in such funds? In fact, why aren't they already doing so? She also advocates for better secondary trading marketplaces for local investors: "It's not super clear what happens if later I want to sell my stock to someone else. . . . It would be really nice if we could have a secondary trading market, if you could buy stock in the café down the street and later sell it and buy stock in a local bookstore."

At any rate, death by interpretation and selective enforcement are the province of bureaucracies. And with all of that "wiggle room," the public should be compelled not to leave matters exclusively in the hands of the government. This concept was fortunately not lost on many motivated parties, and it gave rise to crowdfunding industry-specific associations and self-regulatory organizations (SROs).

The Crowdfund Intermediary Regulatory Advocates (CFIRA)

As of the 2012 time frame, two main American-centric factions developed in the crowdfunding SRO space, both of which have been actively interacting with regulators, lawmakers, platforms, and interested parties. One of the two is the Crowdfund Intermediary Regulatory Advocates (CFIRA).[23] CFIRA sprouted from the Crowdfunding Leadership Group that was mentioned by President Obama at the bill signing ceremony. Sherwood "Woodie" Neiss (who testified in the House of Representatives) and Jason Best, both members of the small team that drove the exemption process, were tasked with gathering the 13 signatories. The group has grown to nearly 100 participants, many of whom are building crowdfunding platforms and want to have their voices represented, as well as security lawyers. Neiss and Best sit on the board in advisory positions, and they are very active in the process. CFIRA has the following stated goal:

> CFIRA will provide U.S. intermediaries with regulation, reporting, and compliance oversight and will provide investors with educational tools to help make more informed decisions about the opportunities and risks of CrowdFund Investing. CFIRA is committed to working with the SEC to create reasonable and appropriate regulations and oversight to reduce fraud and protect investors.

The CFIRA is working with the many involved players, formulating industry standards, including those in a proposed antifraud initiative, that include the following:

1. Funding portal register, similar to Broker-Check. This should allow easy checking for registration status.
2. Whistle-blower program similar to existing programs at the SEC but scaled to the smaller amounts expected.
3. Third-party escrow.
4. Due diligence requirements with these key components:
   a. Background and history check for registrant, scaled to funding amounts
   b. Education of potential investors on crowdfunding generally
   c. Survey investors individually to verify their understanding of the risk they are taking in general and on this particular deal [24]

Demonstrating how dialed-in the CFIRA team is to the intersection of social networking and crowdfunding, the organization issued the following in a news dispatch. One doesn't see this kind of savvy come out of yesteryear's securities regulation bodies:

> The Crowdfund Intermediary Regulatory Advocates organization ("CFIRA") yesterday sent a letter to the SEC highlighting the importance of social media to crowdfund investing. Specifically, the letter proposes that issuers of equity who use the JOBS Act's crowdfunding exemption should be allowed to send "notices"— tweets, Facebook posts, status updates and the like—to potential investors "without being deemed to be engaged in general solicitation.

Crowdfunding Professional Association (CfPA)

Because CFIRA's focus was on SRO-like activities, there was a need for a professional association relevant to the broader crowdfunding industry. Out of this need was born a sister organization, the Crowdfunding Professional Association (CfPA),[25] with the following stated mission:

> The Crowdfunding Professional Association (CfPA) is dedicated to facilitating a vibrant, credible and growing crowdfunding community. CfPA brings together the many voices behind this historic breakthrough in capital creation.

National Crowdfunding Association (NLCFA)

A second faction, the National Crowdfunding Association (NLCFA),[26] launched just prior to the passage of the JOBS Act, with the following expressed mission:

> We are an inclusive trade association of crowdfunding professionals, portals, VC firms, angel investors, attorneys, accountants,

software vendors, educators and students, and many more who are participants in making crowdfunding work. We do/will operate as a traditional trade association, producing an annual trade conference, providing educational materials and opportunities for our members, representing our member body to the applicable regulatory authorities, providing business opportunities uniquely to our members, obtaining and offering group insurance to our members, and so on.[27]

Also among the interesting public comments on the JOBS Act is the NLCFA's memorandum, which formulates what they believe to be the industry's top 24 issues.[28] Both factions have attracted significant interest from many players, and thus it will be an interesting and developing story to watch as things unfold.

Europe

It's only a matter of time before European nations make their own crowdfunding legislation. The JOBS Act set off a wave of competitive spirits. Even before the American legislation passed, various forms of crowdfunding were going full steam across Europe. And the rumblings for regulatory change were already under way. In November 2011, at the AGORADA conference in Bielsko-Biała, Poland, a declaration was signed—essentially a statement from interested parties to the European government, to get the ball rolling:

The Bielsko-Biała Declaration proposes general guidelines for the support of crowdfunding by Member States, Regions, and Cities in order to fully realize the potential of that funding source. It encourages the EC to develop a collaboration framework and knowledge exchange system that facilitates access to information on this new industry and promotes the adoption of common regulations at national level. The Bielsko-Biała Declaration is the outcome of cooperation between Eurada members, Crowdfunding Initiative managers, and the TAKE IT UP Project EVP Team. [29]

Just a few months later in February 2012 came a report from the Association for UK Interactive Entertainment, a trade association representing businesses and organizations in the U.K. games and interactive entertainment industry, entitled *UKIE Crowd Funding Report: A Proposal to Facilitate Crowd Funding in the UK*.[30] After seeing many successful gaming projects launched using crowdfunding, the UKIE proposed a "light touch" regulatory regime. Repeatedly, we see this pattern—those inside the industry get how functional crowdfunding already is and would prefer to have the industry set the pace, and those outside want to regulate it into oblivion.

International

Even if all nations were to legitimize and codify crowdfunding in legislation, that would not guarantee any continuity of standards throughout the industry, and crowdfunding across national borders would be confusing and full of regulatory and legal pitfalls. It's worth pointing out the irony, that the less government regulation imposed on crowdfunding across the board, the easier it is to harmonize practices across countries, allowing the industry associations to more effectively fill in the gaps and deal with national specific issues. Enacting heavy regulation has the net effect of pushing interests to platforms in nations who do choose the "light tough" regulatory regime for crowdfunding, thus ultimately creating a form of "brain drain" along with a drain of capital, innovation, and pretty much everything else desirable.

If you stop and think about it for a moment, best practices are best practices. There are many things that just make sense, regardless of the country in question. For example, having good web security or transparency are good things applied everywhere, whether they're mandated or not. Recognizing this, crowdsourcing.org, an industry go-to site for the larger umbrella field of crowdsourcing, created the Crowdfunding Accreditation for Platform Standards (CAPS) program[31] to promote the adoption of best practices for the operation of crowdfunding platforms globally. With CAPS, accreditation is awarded based on passing qualification criteria in four categories of platform operation:

1. Operational transparency
2. Security of information and payments
3. Platform functionality
4. Operational procedures

Crowdfunding sites can apply to the CAPS program for accreditation, based on an interview and a review process. If they don't make the grade, they can make adjustments and reapply to the program. Whether legally required or not, becoming members of reputable crowdfunding trade organizations and receiving accreditation are ways of signaling a level of credibility to investors, entrepreneurs, and other ecosystems players.

Chapter | 14

REGULATION AND POLICY DIRECTIONS

*And always remember that anything that causes
the shadow is smaller than the source of light.*
—Joseph M. Marshall III[1]

We live in a sea of regulatory irony. It's quite a simple proposition to acquire a $5,000 advance on one's credit card to finance travel, hotel, meals, and a day of gambling in Las Vegas. Unfortunately, debt incurred in Vegas doesn't stay in Vegas, and neither does loss. But if the travel is inconvenient, there's really nothing stopping a person in the United States from spending the same $5,000 gambling on lottery tickets, available nearly everywhere (and there's nearly a 100 percent chance of losing it all). But it is not legal, based on American SEC regulations that exist ostensibly to regulate away the potentials for fraud, to ask the general public to collectively fund a start-up for the same $5,000 amount in, say, $50 per-person increments, in exchange for equity. Even through the lens of a quick order-of-magnitude assessment, say that 1 out of 10 start-ups result in a successful exit, 1 out of 100 include fraud, and winning big in the lottery might occur 1 out of 10 million times, this regulatory situation borders on the ludicrous at best.

Common concerns that people express regarding crowdfunding are of unsophisticated investors' losing all of their money and of potentials for fraudulent fund-raising activities. As a side note, what exactly does a "sophisticated" lottery ticket investor look like? At any rate, while reasonable and quite natural without a larger perspective of crowdfunding, these concerns are not so much bad as they are misdirected. Fraud happens in any system, but if you believe at least in the order-of-magnitude terms previously stated, failure happens way more frequently in start-ups. Be it through fraud or more commonly failure (and we can include lack of producing a DVD and so on in the creative crowdfunding camp as failure), lots of losses will occur. The focus on losing money is grossly misdirected, and it confuses the real issues because the loss of funding in a single project is *not* the problem. It has *never been* the problem. The problem is and has always been the lack of best practices. In this case, the relevant best practice is diversification, and the focus should be on diversifying one's portfolio of money under risk, at least to some reasonable level such that loss can be tolerated. And the second most important best practice is that of offering education to the customers.

The risk-reward curve in the start-up world is quite well established. While it will vary a bit across industries, stages of funding, localities, and other factors, the shape of the curve is extremely similar. Even for early-stage start-ups, there is a wealth of existing data available. In fact, if you're looking for a great summary of exiting data, check out the fabulous research web page at Right Side Capital.[2] At the risk of sounding too general, sometimes investments lose all or some of the money, sometimes they go sideways or make a little bit of return, and only in a single-digit percentage of the time does an investment produce the legendary 10 times return. It doesn't take a PhD in statistics to understand that with those odds (especially of losing most of the investment), it's not good to invest a big percentage of one's total portfolio in any one investment.

And for that matter, it's not good to invest money that a person can't afford to lose. Of course, any crowdfunding platform needs to have checks and balances, which can help reduce fraud wherever possible. But what we're talking about are issues relating to educating investors about high-risk investing and about diversification. Disclosing the historical risk-reward curve is a best practice: the figures are known, simple to graph, and easy to understand, and so they should be conveyed. Offering a small amount of investor education (optional or otherwise) is a best practice. Diversifying is a best practice. At the end of the day, if a crowdfunding platform and any given project seeking funding on that platform makes the proper efforts and facilitates and implements best practices, it's up to the people to then decide how they want to invest their money. Unfortunately, up to now, related regulation has focused on *who* can invest, not *how* people invest, having had the distortive effect of immensely narrowing the size of the crowd—except, that is, if people want to gamble their money away, in which case *everyone* can do that. Downside enjoys freedom; upside, not so much.

Pray for Much Failure

Today, it's impossible to argue against the monumental impact that open source has had on both the innovation ecosystem that it enabled and the landscape of commercial software against which it competes. Yet, as anyone involved in the open source world would confirm, there exists an immense amount of failure. One might think an environment characterized by so much failure would offer little threat to the commercial software industry, but as Clay Shirky in his book *Here Comes Everybody* found, "Open source is a profound threat, not because the open source ecosystem is outsucceeding commercial efforts but because it is outfailing them."[3] If the process of innovation comes with inherent risks, then optimizing against failures comes with a concomitant optimization against success.

And yet many organizations attempt to reduce failure by reducing the odds of its occurring. This is very unfortunate because in doing so, they fail to indulge in one of the divine propositions offered by the Universe: the temporal asymmetry of failure versus success. Simply put, if an organization (or whole ecosystem as in open source) recognizes failures more quickly but it continues to allocate resources to successes, then the returns are much better than a simple ratio of success to failure might suggest. This is even more true at the early stage, whereby the "barriers to exit" (like the tendency of throwing good money after bad) are diminished, making killing off failing projects relatively easier and less complex. At the early stage, failure is cheap.

Failure isn't just an important part of any value creation ecosystem. Lack of it is an indicator of poor health of the ecosystem because it signals that too many constraints have been imposed, and it means that the system has attempted to "cherry pick" a very narrow set of opportunities for success. But there are a number of systemically evil consequences of this. One major consequence is that cherry picking translates to picking "obvious successes." Obviousness tends to occur with either later-term projects or when the future value of potentially successful projects is easier to see (that is, they have been de-risked). In either case, that creates value backwardation in the innovation ecosystem, which is another way of saying that the system is optimizing for less risk. And as stated, any system that optimizes for less risk optimizes for less success.

From a viewpoint of technological innovation, much has been studied about the importance of failure. In fact, refuting the tired axiom that "form follows function," Henry Petroski, engineering professor at Duke University, makes the countercase that "form follows failure" in his book *The Evolution of Useful Things*[4] as well as throughout a number of his other books including *Success Through Failure: The Paradox of Design*.[5] His explanation is best summarized with his statement: "Clever people in the past, whom we today might call inventors, designers, or engineers, observed the failure of existing things to function as well as might be imagined. By focusing on the shortcomings of things, innovators altered those items to remove the imperfections, thus producing new, improved objects."

Thus, not only is failure important to innovation, but *transparency* of failure is tantamount. The higher the number of people observing failure, the more possible solvers there are. This is an exciting prospect for crowdfunding and open innovation alike. Another relevant and equally important observation comes from the paper "Innovation and Selection in Evolutionary Models of Technology," from Joel Mokyr.[6] For true selection (and thus innovation) to occur in an evolutionary system, the system needs *superfecundity*—that is, the system is populated with an excess of options. This creates real competition and forces selection. A healthy amount of failure is necessary for a healthy amount of progress. Incidentally, it's telling when one juxtaposes this necessity for failure with the cry from some in the VC community, "There are too many start-ups being created."

It is for these reasons, that any regulation must *not* regulate for fear of failures and thus *not* for loss of money. Those things will be taken care of largely by diversification and, of course, by the market forces of crowdfunding platforms that facilitate the most value in these areas attracting the most participants.

Taxes, Taxes, Taxes

There are many ways governments can help excite and reinforce crowdfunding's true economic growth potential. It's nearly inescapable to talk about taxation in a discussion about making any economic system more efficient. While most people are still trying to wire around the matrix of hurdles presented to crowdfunding by the regulatory environment, it's never too early to think about taxes.

The following is an idea that could be equally applied to any asset class (and preferably across all assets classes). Using the public equity markets as an analogy (since most people are familiar with them to an extent), it's difficult to see the logic for taxing the "gain" on the sale of a stock if the money is then otherwise to be reinvested in another stock. It's not just that there is no more actual gain to the investors than there would be had they held a stock that had risen in price. This is not only a perversion of the system but it is also a disincentive for investors to reallocate capital to where it belongs, for example, in companies that represent the future. Not all countries have this tax policy, but the ones that do optimize for the wrong outcomes.

A rational and extremely simple way to boost crowdfunding's prospects are to start out fresh with a new and sane taxation model, one that allows investment money to recirculate untaxed within crowdfunding, allowing the economy to gain all of the associated economic multiplier effects, which then generates more tax revenues. It will be promising to see countries implement this.

Patents and Crowdfunding Platforms

A large component of any crowdfunding platform, whether it serves the creative arts, fashion, thrill seekers, or start-ups or otherwise, is its software. Any kind of algorithm and mechanism that enhances a platform's ability to match participants, assess potentials, reduce noise, and so on, obviously brings about a tremendous amount of value to crowdfunding. This was described in Chapter 10, which was dedicated to the idea of using prediction market mechanics to enhance performance of investing within crowdfunding.

But many software techniques are subject to the patent process, at least in the United States. That may well disadvantage crowdfunding in countries that honor "software patents." So it behooves policy makers in various countries to consider the ramifications of patents, possibly eliminating software patents altogether. But beyond that are much broader issues with intellectual property (IP). We've already seen the battle begin, with Kickstarter ensnared by patent claims from the 2000-era fan funding site ArtistShare. And the press release from EquityNet states that it believes it's the first company to patent and develop a crowdfunding platform.[7] And of course, copyright issues are just as thorny for crowdfunding campaigns, including issues surrounding joint works. Much work there needs to be done.

The IP Landscape

In 500 BC, in the Greek city of Sybaris (now southern Italy), a 1-year patent was issued to anyone "who should discover any new refinement in luxury, the profits arising from which were secured to the inventor."[8] In 1449, King Henry VI granted the first 20-year English patent for a method of making stained glass.[9] Given the rates of technological change during those periods of time, reasonable arguments could have been made for the granting of such provisional monopolies of ideas. What's 20 years when a technology generation is 100 years? In the United States, the patent system dates back to the 1770s, but excepting for some oscillation in the term and start date of patents, it has effectively granted 20-year patents for most of its history—the same duration as for the 1449 stained glass patent in England.

If one were to plot two data sets on the same graph versus time, one representing the duration of technology generations (which is decreasing rapidly of late) and a second representing the duration of granted patents (which has remained nearly constant over hundreds of years), then a number of observations become more apparent.

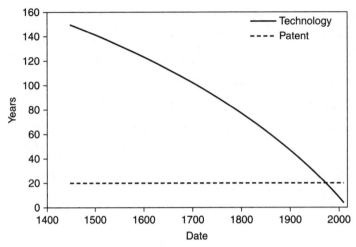

Figure 14.1 The Duration of Technology Generations Versus the Duration of Granted Patents

Figure 14.1 illustrates this relationship, though of course it represents a contrived and monolithic technology generation duration, mostly biased to many of the Internet-derived technologies. Obviously, not all fields have the same rate of change, so feel free to choose your own data for the downtrend in duration of technology generations; the key points remain much the same.

Focusing on more recent innovations, the Commercial Internet Age, as was mentioned, is less than 20 years old. Derivative technologies that have been enabled by the Internet, including many socially oriented technologies, have far shorter generational lives, many in the single digits such as 3, 4, or 5 years. Much of our capacity to innovate stems not just from a rising population but also from the exponential rise in our ability to form more complex connectivities between members of the population, and the related mechanisms that allow for information to be disseminated throughout those connections.

This is one of the key fundamentals of complexity economics, as described by Eric Beinhocker in his book *The Origin of Wealth*.[10]

Just from an observational (that is, a rearview mirror) perspective, it's quite obvious that we've already passed the inflection point where the intellectual property system can possibly well serve innovation. Perhaps the advent of the Commercial Internet Age in the early 1990s served as a waypoint, marking the historical intersection of the patent and the technology generation durations at the 20 years' point. Regardless, we are way past that intersection point now, and it's conceivable that a single patent could hold back multiple technology generations within the patent's lifetime and all of the subsequent derivative innovations. But if patent durability seems lopsided, consider copyrights in the United States, which grant a term equal to an author's life plus an additional 70 years after the author's death![11] Our species might otherwise populate another planet by then.

The Velocity of Innovation and the Effects of the IP System

In economic terms, it's very important to distinguish the *supply of money*, a more static measurement of the amount of various forms of currency in the system, from the *velocity of money*. The *velocity of money* refers to the amount of economic activity occurring in the system, or more generally speaking, how busy the supply of money is in making transactions. If people bury all their cash in their backyards, there's not going to be much velocity of money (and thus not much economic activity). The exact same concept applies to innovation, although this analogy isn't generally made. But it helps paint a very clear picture of the stifling characteristic of our intellectual property system with respect to today's innovation and rate of change.

All of the modern physical and social technologies that have created the complex web of connectivities among our enormous population have essentially enabled a *supply of innovation*, in the spirit of complexity economics. If that supply were allowed to run free, the natural drive ("the animal spirits") of many players in the system would create an enormous *velocity of innovation*. Now consider the intellectual property rights systems of many developed countries: they were set up to handle the complexity economics of circa 1500, or perhaps 1800, but certainly not the twenty-first century.

To add some tangibility, in the United States, it can cost on the order of $15,000 to do a proper patent filing through an IP lawyer. An entrepreneur friend claims he won't bother filing a patent unless he's willing to spend from $50,000 to $70,000 diligencing the "white space" surrounding his patent. And yet, any worthwhile start-up could potentially infringe on hundreds or even thousands of patents. In pragmatic terms, this means that new ventures face two relatively poor options: they can either start off with significant IP litigation risks or never start at all. And if they do start, they are likely to spend a material percentage of their capital fighting through the thicket that covers the intellectual property landscape.

What this means on a macroscale for this next century is that those societies that do well with growth of innovation and derived economic activities will be the ones that also factor in modern intellectual property rights mechanisms, compatible if not symbiotic with inducing a velocity of innovation. There are few categories of technology innovation remaining that are compatible with the current duration of intellectual property rights. Every year, there will be fewer yet.

Unfortunately going forward, what this portends in this hyperconnected world is even more ominous. While the IP-rights-impeded societies will continue to generate more supply of innovation, the wealth stored in that innovation is essentially transferred elsewhere, where it will go on to create velocity and thus economic activity. Attempts at expanding current multilateral IP agreements will only make those nations poorer, and the ones with IP innovation-friendly policies richer. Intellectual property has become largely an unfortunate transfer-of-wealth mechanism, with the transfer going in an unintended direction.

Now consider crowdfunding and pretty much all other forms of crowd-anything and social networking. They are embodiments of complexity economics. They are because, as Paul Romer, Stanford professor of economics and author of "Endogenous Technological Change," has taught us, the very origin of wealth is in finding new means of collaboration.[12] This was also a point made by Yochai Benkler, author of *The Wealth of Networks*: "The opportunities that the network information economy offers, however, often run counter to the central policy drive of both the United States and the European Union in the international trade and intellectual property systems. . . . Chapter 2 explains *why such a policy is suspect* from a purely economic perspective concerned with optimizing innovation" [emphasis mine].[13]

But Benkler also makes an equally important point from a general welfare point of view:

A system that relies too heavily on proprietary approaches to information production is not, however, merely inefficient. It is unjust. Proprietary rights are designed to elicit signals of people's willingness and ability to pay. . . . A system that signals what innovations are most desirable and rations access to these innovations based on ability, as well as willingness, to pay overrepresents welfare gains of the wealthy and underrepresents welfare gains of the poor. Twenty thousand American teenagers can simply afford, and will be willing to pay, much more for acne medication than the more than 1 million Africans who die of malaria every year can afford to pay for a vaccine.[14]

Oddly, as flawed as the analysis would be, patents are often used as a quantitative measure by economists to assess overall innovation.[15] The irony here, especially going forward, is that the number of patents will more realistically and increasingly measure the *inability* for ideas to be converted to actionable innovation, and thus the number of patents will be a measure of the inability to create wealth based on the creation of ideas.

A Perpetual Motion Machine of Innovation

According to the laws of thermodynamics, a perpetual motion machine is an impossibility. If you were to tell people that such a machine existed and it had been created by a government, they'd look for the exit door. Please note where all the exits are. Okay, now imagine an investment fund that invested in new innovative technologies and companies using crowdfunding, and let's assume that fund does quite well—or at least it is profitable and it is able to recycle returns back into new investments. That seems plausible enough, right? It's pretty much Venture Capital meets crowdfunding. Now, what if that's how a nation's R&D budget (for example, grant money) were invested? Conceivably, once the "pump is primed," no new funding (via taxation) is needed, although more could be put in. This is the perpetual motion machine of nationally focused innovation. Fully transparent, accountable, and expressive of the collective will of the people it represents.

One interesting way to float a trial balloon of this concept would be to vector smaller amounts of grant money into funds run by college students to be invested using crowdfunding in important sectors such as clean technology and life sciences. Not only would this add a healthy amount of competition into the mix but it would also be an excellent educational opportunity (including teaching the discipline of investing and fund managing in schools). And why not bring this to the high school level?

EPILOGUE

When it comes to the future, there are three kinds of people:
those who let it happen, those who make it happen,
and those who wonder what happened.
—John Richardson, Jr.

We live in a tropical rainforestlike innovation ecology. The size of our crowd is our diversity, our minds are the soil, and our ideas are the rich nutrients. Now if we can just get to pass us those dark clouds hovering above that are our current regulatory and intellectual property realities, when the light shines down here, we're going to have growth in a way this planet has never seen.

It's important to look back at history for a moment, at a time when massive socioeconomic changes occurred, for some key sights moving forward. The first Industrial Revolution, characterized by the mechanization enabled largely by the steam engine, took place in some countries for the good part of a century. What's critical to contemplate isn't just the immense change that took place but how different the industrialization played out in various countries. In some it lagged by *many* decades.

While there were myriad related factors (differences in natural resources, culture, rule, and so on), there was one absolutely key and hard-to-refute aspect of this incongruity: the transfer of knowledge. New inventions led to mechanized factories in England, arguably an origin of the first Industrial Revolution. However, England fought to keep its industrialization edge, prohibiting factory workers from leaving the country in an attempt to prevent the transfer of related technological knowledge. That alone is thought to have retarded the spread of industrialization by decades. But what is more telling are the circumstances that are well evidenced surrounding the patenting of the steam engine by James Watt in London in 1769.

Not much happened by way of production for years. But Watt's business partner, the influential industrialist Matthew Boulton, helped secure an act of Parliament extending his patent until the year 1800. While the fuel efficiency of steam engines changed little during the life of Watt's patent, it increased an estimated factor of five between 1810 and 1835, during which time, "steam power came into its own as the driving force of the Industrial Revolution."[1] Ironically, Watt could not use a key mechanical configuration, the crank and flywheel, to improve the efficiency of his steam engine design because it relied on a method patented by James Pickard. Mankind waits decades, or even centuries at times, for the storm clouds to pass.

It's not at all obvious which countries will emerge as leaders in this next period of revolutionary change. Massive change does not favor the previous pecking order. It may be that the new leaders will appear to have been very unlikely candidates, indeed. But no matter, they will be the ones who understand that our value stems from the amazing social complexity that our world now offers. We are in the third phase of what Thomas Malone in *The Future of Work* speaks of: we are in a natural transition to intellectual decentralization. The power of our complexity economics derives from the web of our interactions. Those who encourage, embrace, and if nothing else, just get out of the way will emerge as leaders.

Ideas are just that, until people act on them. They are part of the immense *idea supply*, which we could analogize to the natural mineral resources on Earth. When they are mined, processed, and shaped into something productive, then they create social and economic benefits, which beget the further advancement of ideas. This is the concept of the *velocity of innovation*. With the increasing connectedness we enjoy, the idea supply will keep growing, although the economically stimulating velocity of innovation may be very incongruous across various countries. If the nations that enriched themselves with the spoils of leading the previous industrialization are not quick to adapt to the new revolutionary forces, then history may well record a provocative irony: newer developing nations may effectively be mining or otherwise exploiting the idea supply resources of previously developed nations.

In his book *Operating Manual for Spaceship Earth* (circa 1968),[2] Buckminster Fuller states: "We find that the physical constituent of wealth—energy—cannot decrease and that the metaphysical constituent—know-how—can only increase. This is to say that every time we use our wealth it increases." As such, there is no such thing as systemic wealth *deflation*, although given enough influence, wealth can be *redistributed* unnaturally. The only remedies to this are transformations that allow the creation of wealth to revert back to natural distribution—and to those who provide true value. Crowdfunding is one embodiment of the system's self-administered remedy. And so the economic irony is that our future depends less on what governments do to widen the path for crowdfunding than on how much they get out of our way.

We sincerely hope you've enjoyed sharing our journey. It's good to have you as part of the G-7 Billion. As crowdfunding becomes incrementally part of our new ritual, many new opportunities will arise along with new questions, which we hope you'll ask. But for now, here are a few things to ponder, to get the creative juices flowing:

1. *Search:* What will "search" look like for crowdfunding? Who will be the "Google" of this space?
2. *Meta-sites:* How long before there are meta-sites for crowdfunding that provide "one-stop shopping" for funding of projects across many of the individual sites? What about for trends and analytics?
3. *Human versus the machine:* Will we create algorithms and use prediction markets to make early picks of winning start-ups? The picks that resulted would be better than many manmade picks (as has been achieved in chess)?
4. *Crowd Street:* There's Main Street and Wall Street. What will a mature Crowd Street look like?
5. *Communities:* What will be the first community to use crowdfunding to do all of their budget planning?
6. *Biotech:* A recent supercomputer experiment beat previous records in protein folding by a factor of over 100.[3] Will crowdfunding plus cloud computing yield the next biotech giant?
7. *Animation studios:* Specialized render-farms were, until now, the standard. But the trend, starting with providers like PEER 1 Hosting,[4] is to move high-performance graphics and scientific computing to the cloud. Server-side gaming is also moving to the cloud. Will the next major new animation studio be cloud based, and thus, could it be crowdfunded?
8. *Countries:* Will the first countries to materially empower crowdfunding be the next powerhouse innovation centers in the world?
9. *Sovereign wealth funds:* Which will be the first country to have a sovereign wealth fund that invests in crowdfunding?
10. *Fan funding:* Will the next Lance Armstrong be sponsored through fan funding via a site like ThrillCapital?

11. *Proprietary or open source platforms:* Which will win out, proprietary or open source platforms? How do white-box and cobranding strategies fit into the future?

12. *Team matching:* How long before team matching algorithms and services help coalesce teams?

13. *Cooperatives:* Will cooperatives become a popular investment in our portfolios?

14. *Asset class for crowds:* Will there be a new "crowd class" of equity created to ensure compatibility with downstream professional investors?

15. *Fees for crowdfunding:* What payment paradigm will shake up the relatively high fees involved with crowdfunding?

16. *P2P and alternative currencies:* Will crowdfunding soon integrate with P2P, alternate currencies, and natural peer technologies?

17. *Universal language translation for crowds:* Will crowdsourced universal language translation (for example, Babelverse[5]) make crowdfunding a truly global thing?

18. *Investment standards:* Will exchange-traded funds (ETFs) and mutual funds for start-ups and local businesses become the investment standards? Will they be possible in retirement savings vehicles?

19. *Local stock exchanges:* Will we see a return to local stock exchanges as a result of crowdfunding?

20. *Crowdfunding apps:* Will a crowdfunding platform become the "next Facebook"? Will it have an app market?

21. *Mission to Mars:* Humans landed on the moon about eight years after President Kennedy's famous 1961 speech. As the United States canceled its Constellation program that called for a return to the moon by 2020, could a large internationally coordinated crowdfunding effort land humans on Mars by 2020 instead? Note that SpaceX's successful Falcon 9 rocket launch proved how capital efficient spaceflight can be.

The entire system was built for less than the cost of the service tower for the National Aeronautics and Space Administration's (NASA's) proposed spaceflight vehicle!

Danny Hillis, in his book *The Pattern on the Stone: The Simple Ideas That Make Computers Work*, made the incredibly powerful and prescient prediction: "The greatest achievement of our technology may well be the creation of tools that allow us to go beyond engineering—that allow us to create more than we can understand."[6] What is upon us are all the necessary ingredients for just that to occur and on a massive socioeconomic scale. Ironically, many of our biggest current challenges center around the undoing of dysfunctional constraints, largely artificially imposed on us. These constraints come namely from the ideologies that tell us that thought and intellectual processes are property and that free speech is dangerous.

Well, bad ideologies may not die easily. Rather, they often get marginalized into irrelevancy. In the evolution of a race is the transition from intense and brutal competition to constructive cooperation. We are in that moment. What we create will go beyond us. And as a result, our race will go beyond.

Engage!

—Kevin and Dan

NOTES

Introduction

1. "Crowdfunding," *Wikipedia*, http://en.wikipedia.org/wiki/Crowd_funding, accessed in 2010.
2. Internet World Stats, "Internet Usage Statistics: The Internet Big Picture," http://www.internetworldstats.com/stats.htm, accessed in 2010.
3. Neatorama, "The True Story of the Statue of Liberty," May 31, 2007, http://www.neatorama.com/2007/05/31/the-true-story-of-the-statue-of-liberty/.
4. Ibid.
5. Antti Hannula, "The Statue of Liberty Was Crowdfunded," Insider's View to Entrepreneurship, Gasellit, October 13, 2010.
6. Peter Drucker, *Postcapital*, June 9, 2009, http://www.postcapital.org/2009/01/09/the-post-capitalist-society/.

Chapter 1

1. *Infoplease, Columbia Electronic Encyclopedia*, 6th ed., Columbia University Press, 2007, http://www.infoplease.com/ce6/history/A0821954.html.
2. "Crowdsourcing," *Wikipedia*, http://en.wikipedia.org/wiki/Crowdsourcing.
3. As attributed to S. R. Charles, 2007, *Wikianswers*, http://wiki.answers.com/Q/Who_said_the_famous_quote_birds_of_a_feather_flock_together.
4. Microsoft, http://www.microsoft.com/opensource/, accessed in 2010.
5. Peer To Patent project, at http://www.peertopatent.org/.
6. Algodeal, http://algodeal.com/.
7. CrowdConf, http://www.crowdconf.com/.
8. Crowdsortium, http://www.crowdsortium.org.
9. Kenneth Bausch, "Harnessing Collective Wisdom and Power," http://www.harnessingcollectivewisdom.com/syllabus.html, accessed in 2010.
10. Yochai Benkler, *The Wealth of Networks*, Yale University Press, New Haven, CT, 2006, http://cyber.law.harvard.edu/wealth_of_networks/Main_Page.
11. Eric D. Beinhocker, *The Origin of Wealth*, McKinsey & Company, New York, 2006, p. 244.
12. Ibid., p. 262.
13. Ibid., p. 246.
14. Chris Ward, http://www.ward.is/.

15. Jonathan Gosier, September 7, 2010, http://blog.ushahidi.com/index. php/2010/10/07/crowdsourcing-and-chaos-theory/.
16. "Virtual Business," *Wikipedia*, David R. Johnson, 2008, http://en.wikipedia. org/wiki/Virtual_business.
17. Stuart Dredge, "Liveblog: Facebook's Joanna Shields: Engaging Audiences Through Social Networking," *mipblog*, October 5, 2010, http://blog. mipworld.com/2010/10/liveblog-facebooks-joanna-shields-on-engaging-your-audience-through-social-media/.
18. "Mashup," *Wikipedia*, http://en.wikipedia.org/wiki/ Mashup_%28web_application_hybrid%29.
19. Charles Leadbeater and Paul Miller, *The Pro-Am Revolution*, pamphlet, Demos publications, London, November 24, 2004, http://www.demos.co.uk/ publications/proameconomy.
20. Robert D. Putnam, *Bowling Alone*, Simon & Schuster, New York, 2000, http://www.bowlingalone.com/.
21. Benkler, *Wealth of Networks*, p. 138.
22. "Virtual Business," *Wikipedia*, "What Is a Vermont Virtual Company?" http://en.wikipedia.org/wiki/Virtual_business.
23. Alan Rappeport, "Vermont Wants to Be the 'Delaware of the Net,'" *CFO*, June 30, 2008, http://www.cfo.com/article.cfm/11654091.

Chapter 2

1. National Research Council Canada, *Converging Technologies and New Product Markets*, Roundtable VIII Report, April 28–29, 2003, http://dsp-psd. pwgsc.gc.ca/Collection/NR16-74-2003E.pdf.
2. "Generation," *Wikipedia*, http://en.wikipedia.org/wiki/Generation.
3. James Surowiecki, *The Wisdom of Crowds*, First Anchor Books, New York, 2005, p. 35.
4. *PuneTech*, September 2009, http://punetech.com/tech-trends-for-2015-by-anand-deshpande-shridhar-shukla-monish-darda/, accessed in 2010.
5. Robin Wauters, *TechCrunch*, October 10, 2010, http://techcrunch. com/2010/10/06/steve-jobs-mark-zuckerberg-teens/.
6. http://www.southparkstudios.com/.
7. http://www.themedicigroup.com/the-medici-effect.
8. Paul Graham, August 2010, http://www.paulgraham.com/future.html.
9. Liz Gannes, July 2010, http://gigaom.com/2010/07/29/. how-y-combinator-is-remaking-silicon-valley-in-its-image/.
10. Evelyn Rusli, second video listed, July 2010, http://techcrunch. com/2010/07/30/paul-grahams-checklist-would-you-make-the-cut-video/.
11. Shuba Swaminathan, November 19, 2009, http://entrepreneurs-journal. blogspot.com/2009/11/eric-ries-on-lean-start-ups-mit-talk-on.html.
12. Robert Scoble, November 13, 2009, http://scobleizer.com/2009/11/13/ the-worst-things-startups-do/.
13. Paul Graham, March 2007, http://www.paulgraham.com/notnot.html.

Chapter 3

1. Malcolm Gladwell, *Outliers: The Story of Success*, Little, Brown, New York, 2008, p. 81.
2. Ibid., p. 76.

3. "Millionaire Dropouts," http://web.archive.org/web/20101022051802/http://www.millionairedropouts.com/millionaire.php/Dropout_Trivia/.
4. Nassim Nicholas Taleb, *The Black Swan*, 2d ed., Random House, New York, 2010, http://en.wikipedia.org/wiki/Nassim_Nicholas_Taleb.
5. http://www.tripbod.com/.
6. http://www.missionmission.org/2011/10/26/lending-libraries-arrive-in-the-mission/.
7. http://www.springwise.com/style_design/crowdfunded-bridge-long-citizens-pay/.
8. http://enablingcity.com/.
9. http://www.indiegogo.com/blog/2011/01/whats-new-in-2011-partnerships.html.
10. http://www.kickstarter.com/blog/introducing-curated-pages.

Chapter 4

1. Y Combinator, http://ycombinator.com/.
2. Stanford Student Startup Accelerator (StartX), http://sselabs.stanford.edu/.
3. Venture Company, http://venturecompany.com/.
4. "Tribble," *Wikipedia*, http://en.wikipedia.org/wiki/Tribble.
5. Ted Wang, *VentureBeat*, September 17, 2007, http://venturebeat.com/2007/09/17/reinventing-the-series-a/.
6. Anthony Ha, *VentureBeat*, August 13, 2008, http://venturebeat.com/2008/08/13/cut-your-legal-fees-with-y-combinators-legal-documents/.
7. Anthony Ha, *VentureBeat*, March 2, 2010, http://venturebeat.com/2010/03/02/series-seed-andreessen-horowitz/.

Chapter 5

1. Blender Foundation, http://www.blender.org/.
2. Blender Foundation, *Sintel* page, http://www.sintel.org/.
3. Janko Roettgers, "Blender Foundation Releases Open Source Movie *Sintel*," NewTeeVee column, October 1, 2010, http://newteevee.com/2010/10/01/blender-foundation-releases-open-source-movie-sintel/.
4. Energia Productions, *Star Wreck* page, http://www.starwreck.com/.
5. Energia Productions, *Iron Sky* page, http://www.ironsky.net/.
6. http://www.kickstarter.com/projects/597507018/pebble-e-paper-watch-for-iphone-and-android.
7. http://www.bizjournals.com/sanfrancisco/feature/pebble.html.
8. "Crowdfunding," *Word Spy*, http://www.wordspy.com/words/crowdfunding.asp.
9. Mike Masnick, "The Answer to the $200 Million Movie Question," *Techdirt*, May 16, 2006, http://www.techdirt.com/articles/20060515/0321220.shtml.
10. Hugh Hart, "Space Nazi Trailers Draw Crowd Funding for *Iron Sky*," *Wired*, June 29, 2010, http://www.wired.com/underwire/2010/06/iron-sky-space-nazis/.
11. http://www.marioarmstrong.com/2012/05/17/video-interview-with-pebble-watch-founder-eric-migicovsky-the-brain-behind-the-10-million-kickstarter/.
12. Betty Hallock, "Kickstarter's Growing Grass-Roots Food Scene," *Los Angeles Times*, October 7, 2010, http://www.latimes.com/features/food/la-fo-kickstarter-20101007,0,2499632.story.
13. Long Beach Local, http://www.longbeachlocal.org/.
14. Music Securities, http://www.musicsecurities.com/.

15. 33needs, http://blog.33needs.com/, accessed in 2010.
16. Open Genius, http://www.opengenius.org/.
17. http://www.mediabistro.com/mediajobsdaily/
american-public-media-acquires-journo-crowdfunding-site-spot-us_b9222.
18. http://www.siliconvalleywatcher.com/mt/archives/2012/01/
startupwatch_ar.php.
19. http://www.technologyreview.com/article/40244/.
20. http://www.google.com/trends/?q=crowdfunding.
21. http://howardleonhardt.nationbuilder.com/howardleonhardt/
the_enormous_implications_of_crowdfunding.
22. http://idealab.talkingpointsmemo.com/2012/02/kickstarter-expects-to-
provide-more-funding-to-the-arts-than-nea.php.
23. http://offbeatr.com/.
24. http://www.gogofantasy.com/.
25. Thomas W. Malone, *The Future of Work*, Harvard Business School Press,
Boston, 2004, http://ccs.mit.edu/futureofwork/.
26. "Do it yourself," *Wikipedia*, http://en.wikipedia.org/wiki/Do_it_yourself,
accessed in 2010.
27. Antti Hannula, "The Statue of Liberty Was Crowdfunded," Insider's View to
Entrepreneurship, Gasellit, October 13, 2010.
28. PirateMyFilm, http://www.piratemyfilm.com/pages/how_it_works, accessed
in 2010.
29. Internet World Stats, "Usage and Population Statistics, http://www.
internetworldstats.com/eu/nl.htm, accessed in 2010.
30. http://www.crowdaboutnow.com/.
31. World Bank, http://data.worldbank.org/indicator/IT.NET.USER.
P2?cid=GPD_44, accessed in 2010.
32. J. B. Handelsman, *New Yorker*, May 13, 1972, http://archives.newyorker.
com/?i=1972-05-13.
33. Ward Farnsworth, *The Legal Analyst*, University of Chicago Press, Chicago,
2007, http://www.thelegalanalyst.com/.
34. James Surowiecki, 2005, http://conferences.oreillynet.com/cs/et2005/
view/e_sess/7022.
35. SharesPost, http://www.sharespost.com/, accessed in 2010.
36. SecondMarket Holdings, http://www.secondmarket.com/markets/private-
company-stock.html, accessed in 2010.
37. Private Equity Exchange, http://www.peqx.com/, accessed in 2010.
38. http://papers.ssrn.com/sol3/papers.cfm?abstract_id=1028592.
39. http://www.nesta.org.uk/library/documents/Report%2021%20-%20
Business%20Angel%20Inv%20v11.pdf.
40. http://www.huffingtonpost.com/kevin-lawton/democratizing-venture-
cap_b_792498.html.
41. "Glass ceiling," *Wikipedia*, http://en.wikipedia.org/wiki/Glass_ceiling.

Chapter 6

1. http://www.finestquotes.com/quote-id-13959.htm.
2. http://cfsinnovation.com/system/files/09-11,%20Marketscan_final.pdf.
3. http://www.brainyquote.com/quotes/quotes/b/bobhope161800.html.
4. http://www.indiegogo.com/blog/2011/03/crowdfunding-for-filmmakers-
strategies-tactics-pitfalls.html.

5. Stan Davis, *Future Perfect*, Addison-Wesley, Reading, MA, 1996, http://www.amazon.com/Future-Perfect-Tenth-Anniversary-Edition/dp/0201327953/.
6. http://hbr.org/1997/01/the-four-faces-of-mass-customization/ar/.
7. http://wi1.uni-erlangen.de/sites/wi1.uni-erlangen.de/files/Piller_Moeslein_Stotko_PPC_2004_Does_Mass_Customization_Pay.pdf.
8. http://www.indiegogo.com/blog/2011/03/crowdfunding-for-filmmakers-strategies-tactics-pitfalls.html.
9. http://www.ted.com/talks/simon_sinek_how_great_leaders_inspire_action.html.
10. http://www.jamesvictore.com/.
11. http://www.indiegogo.com/blog/2010/04/5-ways-crowdfunding-helps-leverage-grant-support.html.
12. Randy Komisar, *The Monk and the Riddle*, Harvard Business School Press, Boston, http://www.amazon.com/The-Monk-Riddle-Creating-Making/dp/1578516447.
13. http://www.launch.co/.
14. http://www.launch.co/blog/the-two-most-important-startups-in-the-world.html.
15. http://www.trendsresearch.com/predictions/TopTrends2012.pdf.
16. http://papers.ssrn.com/sol3/papers.cfm?abstract_id=1699183.
17. http://www.techtransferonline.com/articles/DisruptiveTechnologiesCatchingtheWave.html.
18. http://www.forbes.com/sites/stevedenning/2011/11/18/clayton-christensen-how-pursuit-of-profits-kills-innovation-and-the-us-economy/.
19. http://www.kickstarter.com/blog/current-events.
20. http://www.aciamericas.coop/2012United-Nations-International.
21. http://www.indiegogo.com/Atlantis-Books.

Chapter 7

1. http://tinybuddha.com/quotes/tiny-wisdom-on-asking-for-help/.
2. Gabor Maté, *In the Realm of Hungry Ghosts*, North Atlantic Books, Berkeley, CA, 2010, http://drgabormate.com/writings/books/in-the-realm-of-hungry-ghosts/.
3. http://www.kpfa.org/archive/id/80433 @ 28:35.
4. http://www.sec.gov/answers/form10q.htm.
5. http://www.kickstarter.com/projects/jokeandbiagio/dying-to-do-letterman-kickstarter-for-an-oscar-and.
6. http://www.dyingtodoletterman.com/.
7. James Victore, *Victore or, Who Died and Made You Boss?*, Abrams, New York, 2010, http://www.amazon.com/gp/product/0810995913.
8. http://the99percent.com/articles/7164/Op-Ed-Confidence-vs-Shyness.
9. http://www.ted.com/talks/louie_schwartzberg_nature_beauty_gratitude.html.
10. http://www.kickstarter.com/blog/the-importance-of-video.
11. http://www.geekindustrialcomplex.com/articles/crowdfunding-report-part-1.
12. http://www.huffingtonpost.com/slava-rubin/indiegogo-founder-crowdfu_b_903627.html.
13. http://www.kickstarter.com/projects/amandapalmer/amanda-palmer-the-new-record-art-book-and-tour.
14. "Three-point lighting," *Wikipedia*, http://en.wikipedia.org/wiki/Three-point_lighting.
15. http://www.huffingtonpost.com/slava-rubin/indiegogo-founder-crowdfu_b_903627.html.

16. http://www.cbinsights.com/blog/venture-capital/ venture-capital-human-capital-report.

17. http://www.boop.org/jan/justso/elephant.htm.

18. Andrea Ordanini, Lucia Miceli, Marta Pizzetti, and A. Parasuraman, "Crowdfunding: Transforming Customers into Investors Through Innovative Service Platforms," Crowdsourcing.org, p. 25, http://www.crowdsourcing. org/document/crowdfunding-transforming-customers-into-investors-through-innovative-service-platforms-/5214.

19. http://garyploski.com/rising-star-the-movie-kickstarter-campaign-review.

20. http://www.kickstarter.com/projects/ryanbkoo/man-child-feature-film.

21. http://nofilmschool.com/2011/08/ ten-must-read-posts-embarking-crowdfunding/.

22. http://www.kickstarter.com/projects/66710809/double-fine-adventure.

23. http://www.kickstarter.com/projects/1104350651/ tiktok-lunatik-multi-touch-watch-kits.

24. http://www.scribd.com/doc/92834651/ Massolution-abridged-Crowd-Funding-Industry-Report.

25. Ajay Agrawal, Christian Catalini, and Avi Goldfarb, "The Geography of Crowdfunding," NET Institute Working Paper No. 10-08, October 29, 2010, p. 13, http://papers.ssrn.com/sol3/papers.cfm?abstract_id=1692661.

26. http://www.forbes.com/sites/alanhall/2012/05/20/ more-questions-on-crowdfunding-industry-research-with-carl-esposti/.

27. http://www.pocketgamer.biz/r/PG.Biz/War+Balloon+Games+news/news. asp?c=39988.

Chapter 8

1. http://www.joyofquotes.com/journey_of_life_quotes.html.

2. "Leave It to Beaver," *Wikipedia*, https://en.wikipedia.org/wiki/ Leave_It_to_Beaver.

3. http://ecorner.stanford.edu/authorMaterialInfo.html?mid=2288.

4. http://www.indiegogo.com/blog/2011/03/crowdfunding-for-filmmakers-strategies-tactics-pitfalls.html.

5. Chris Jones and Genevieve Jolliffe, *The Guerilla Film Makers Handbook*, 3rd ed., Continuum, New York, 2006, http://www.amazon.com/ Guerilla-Film-Makers-Handbook-3e/dp/082647988X.

6. http://www.indiegogo.com/blog/2011/03/crowdfunding-for-filmmakers-strategies-tactics-pitfalls.html.

7. http://filmcourage.com/content/networking-novice-social-maven-how-crowd-funding-and-social-networking-made-me-better.

8. http://www.kickingitforward.org/.

9. http://www.doublefine.com/dfa/.

Chapter 9

1. Marc Andreessen at Stanford Entrepreneurial Thought Leaders Lecture Series, May 12, 2010, http://www.stanford.edu/group/edcorner/uploads/ podcast/andreessen100512.mp3.

2. TheFunded, http://thefunded.com/.

3. CrunchBase, http://www.crunchbase.com/.
4. NYPPEX Private Markets, http://www.nyppex.com/.
5. *Business Wire*, 2001, http://www.prnewswire.com/news-releases-test/nyppe-closes-acquisition-of-offroad-capital-inc-73624957.html?utm_expid=43414375-18.
6. PRIMARQ, http://www.primarq.com/.
7. Indiegogo, http://www.indiegogo.com/.
8. Clay Shirky, *Here Comes Everybody*, Penguin, New York, 2008, p. 125.
9. Ibid., p. 118.
10. Ibid., p. 181.
11. Kevin Lawton, *TrendCaller*, March 8, 2010, http://www.trendcaller.com/2010/03/coming-finders-economy-intermediation.html.
12. Right Side Capital Management, http://rightsidecapital.com/.
13. Ibid.
14. Jeff Howe, *Crowdsourcing*, Three Rivers Press, New York, 2009, p. 145.
15. Paul Graham, "Want to Start a Startup?" August 2010, http://www.paulgraham.com/future.html.
16. Liz Gannes, *GigaOM*, July 29, 2010, http://gigaom.com/2010/07/29/how-y-combinator-is-remaking-silicon-valley-in-its-image/.
17. Evelyn Rusli, *TechCrunch*, July 30, 2010, http://techcrunch.com/2010/07/30/paul-grahams-checklist-would-you-make-the-cut-video/, 2nd video.
18. Kevin Lawton, *VentureBeat*, May 4, 2010, http://venturebeat.com/2010/05/04/the-new-face-of-venture-capital-a-road-map-for-entrepreneurs/, slide 33.
19. International Organization of CrowdFunding Commissions (IOCFC), LinkedIn group, http://www.linkedin.com/groups?mostPopular=&gid=3251311, accessed in 2010.
20. "XBRL," *Wikipedia*, http://en.wikipedia.org/wiki/XBRL.
21. International Organization of CrowdFunding Commissions (IOCFC), LinkedIn group.

Chapter 10

1. Jeff Howe, *Crowdsourcing*, Three Rivers Press, New York, 2009, p. 138.
2. Ibid., p. 151.
3. Ronald S. Burt, "Social Origins of Good Ideas," January 2003, http://www.upcomillas.es/personal/rgimeno/doctorado/SOGI.pdf.
4. Clay Shirky, *Here Comes Everybody*, Penguin, New York, 2008, p. 230.
5. Howe, *Crowdsourcing*, p. 152.
6. John Seely Browd and Paul Duguid, *The Social Life of Information*, Harvard Business School Press, Boston, 2002, http://people.ischool.berkeley.edu/~duguid/SLOFI/.
7. James Surowiecki, *The Wisdom of Crowds*, First Anchor Book, New York, 2005, p. 22.
8. Intrade, http://www.intrade.com/.
9. Friedrich A. Hayek, "The Use of Knowledge in Society," *American Economic Review*, vol. 35, no. 4, 1945, http://www.econlib.org/library/Essays/hykKnw1.html.
10. *Spencer Trask Blog*, http://www.wired.com/magazine/2010/05/ff_pink_shirky/.

11. Michael Nystrom, "Goldcorp, *Wikinomics*, and Changing the World," January 19, 2007, http://www.bullnotbull.com/archive/wikinomics.html.
12. Ibid.
13. Ibid.
14. Shirky, *Here Comes Everybody*, p. 254.
15. "Moore's law," *Wikipedia*, http://en.wikipedia.org/wiki/Moore%27s_law.
16. Kermit Pattison, "How to Kill and Idea," *FastCompany*, May 30, 2008, http://www.fastcompany.com/articles/2008/05/interview-ram-charan.html.
17. YouNoodle, http://younoodle.com/.
18. Jason Kincaid, "Outlook Not So Good: Predictify Heads to the Deadpool," *TechCrunch*, August 7, 2009, http://techcrunch.com/2009/08/07/outlook-not-so-good-predictify-heads-to-the-deadpool/.
19. http://inklingmarkets.com/.
20. Michael Arrington, "Ron Conway's Confidential Investment Guide: The Tech Megatrends," *TechCrunch*, September 13, 2010, http://techcrunch.com/2010/09/13/ron-conways-confidential-investment-guide-the-tech-megatrends/.
21. Scott Kirsner, *Inventing the Movies*, CinemaTech Books, 2008, http://www.scottkirsner.com/inventing/.
22. Zocalo, http://zocalo.sourceforge.net/, accessed in 2010.
23. Open Prediction Markets, http://openpredictionmarkets.org/, accessed in 2010.
24. Kevin Lawton, "46 Percent IRR, Crowd-Enhanced Angel Returns and the Future of Crowdfunding," February 1, 2011, http://www.trendcaller.com/2011/02/46-irr-crowd-enhanced-angel-returns-and.html.
25. Ewing Marion Kauffman Foundation, *Angel Investor Performance Project*, http://sites.kauffman.org/aipp/.
26. AngelList, http://angel.co/jobs-act.
27. Tom Stein, "Funding Bill Stirs the Crowd, *Venture Capital Journal*, February 2012, p. 3, http://privatemarkets.thomsonreuters.com/Venture-capital-journal/.

Chapter 12

1. Grow VC, http://www.growvc.com/main/press/GrowVCAndIndiaCo2010-07-06.pdf, accessed in 2010.
2. Kevin Lawton, *VentureBeat*, 2010, http://venturebeat.com/?s=kevin+lawton.
3. Kevin Lawton, "The New Face of Venture Capital: Crowdfunding's Big Bang," *VentureBeat*, July 6, 2010, http://venturebeat.com/2010/07/06/the-new-face-of-venture-capital-crowdfundings-big-bang/.
4. Cofundit, http://www.cofundit.com/.
5. "Exchange-traded fund," *Wikipedia*, http://en.wikipedia.org/wiki/Exchange-traded_fund.
6. Lawton, "The New Face of Venture Capital."
7. kaChing, now Wealthfront, https://www.wealthfront.com/.
8. Colbert Nation, Comedy Central, http://www.colbertnation.com/.
9. Open Genius, http://www.opengenius.org/.
10. Robert D. Putnam, *Bowling Alone*, Simon & Schuster, New York, 2000, http://www.bowlingalone.com/.

Chapter 13

1. J. DeCecco and A. Richards, *Growing Pains: Uses of School Conflict*, Aberdeen Press, New York, 1974.
2. http://www.washingtonpost.com/blogs/on-small-business/post/small-business-panel-talks-crowdfunding-contracting-and-cupcakes/2012/05/24/gJQAGCJvnU_blog.html.
3. http://www.huffingtonpost.com/kevin-lawton/crowdfunding-fraud-bogey_b_1119101.html.
4. Kauffman Foundation Research Series, *Firm Formation and Economic Growth: The Importance of Startups in Job Creation and Job Destruction*, July 2010, http://www.kauffman.org/uploadedfiles/firm_formation_importance_of_startups.pdf.
5. Amy Cortese, *Locavesting*, Wiley, New York, 2011, http://locavesting.com/Locavesting_homepage.html.
6. Michael Shuman, *Local Dollars, Local Sense*, Post Carbon Institute, White River Junction, VT, http://www.amazon.com/Local-Dollars-Sense-Prosperity--A-Resilience/dp/1603583432/.
7. Michael Shuman, *The Small-Mart Revolution: How Local Businesses Are Beating the Global Competition*, Berrett-Koehler Publishers, San Francisco, 2006, http://www.amazon.com/The-Small-Mart-Revolution-Competition-ebook/dp/B005M0D046.
8. Christine Wong, "Legalize Crowdfunding or Risk Losing Startups to U.S., CATA says," *itbusiness*, February 2, 2012, p. 182, http://www.itbusiness.ca/it/client/en/home/News.asp?id=65909.
9. http://online.wsj.com/article/SB10001424052702304023504577319633228452236.html#slide/1.
10. http://gigaom.com/2012/05/22/kickstarter-founder-perry-chen-intervie/.
11. http://www.crunchbase.com/company/kickstarter.
12. http://www.gpo.gov/fdsys/pkg/PLAW-112publ106/pdf/PLAW-112publ106.pdf.
13. "Securities Act of 1933," *Wikipedia*, https://en.wikipedia.org/wiki/Securities_Act_of_1933.
14. "Securities Exchange Act of 1934," *Wikipedia*, https://en.wikipedia.org/wiki/Securities_Exchange_Act_of_1934.
15. http://www.usconstitution.net/const.html.
16. http://fundinglaunchpad.com/2012/04/investment-crowdfunding-legislation-review/.
17. http://www.businessweek.com/articles/2012-05-24/lobbying-to-become-lobbyists-for-crowdfunding.
18. http://www.usconstitution.net/const.html.
19. http://www.sec.gov/comments/jobs-title-iii/jobstitleiii-39.pdf.
20. http://www.sec.gov/spotlight/jobsactcomments.shtml.
21. http://cuttingedgecapital.com/.
22. http://www.shareable.net/blog/crowdfunding-goes-prime-time-%E2%80%94-what-next.
23. http://www.cfira.org/.
24. http://www.prweb.com/releases/2012/5/prweb9543941.htm.
25. http://crowdfundingprofessional.org/.
26. http://www.nlcfa.org/.
27. http://www.nlcfa.org/about.html.
28. http://www.sec.gov/comments/jobs-title-iii/jobstitleiii-64.pdf.

29. http://www.eurada.org/files/Bielsko-Biala%20Declaration.pdf.
30. http://ukie.org.uk/sites/default/files/UKIE%20Crowd%20Funding%20
Report%20-%20A%20Proposal%20to%20Facilitate%20Crowd%20
Funding%20in%20the%20UK%20-%20%20February%202012.pdf.
31. http://www.crowdsourcing.org/caps.

Chapter 14

1. http://www.livinglifefully.com/fear.htm.
2. Right Side Capital Management (RSCM), http://rightsidecapital.com/
research.html, accessed in 2010.
3. Clay Shirky, *Here Comes Everybody*, Penguin, New York, 2008, p. 245.
4. Henry Petroski, *The Evolution of Useful Things*, Random House,
New York, 1994, http://www.randomhouse.com/catalog/display.
pperl?isbn=9780679740391.
5. Henry Petroski, *Success Through Failure: The Paradox of Design*, Princeton
University Press, Princeton, NJ, 2008, http://press.princeton.edu/titles/8132.
html.
6. Joel Mokyr, "Innovation and Selection in Evolutionary Models of
Technology," 1997, http://faculty.wcas.northwestern.edu/~jmokyr/Ziman.pdf.
7. http://www.prnewswire.com/news-releases/equitynet-first-company-to-patent-
and-develop-crowdfunding-platform-144429485.html
8. "Patent," *Wikipedia*, http://en.wikipedia.org/wiki/Patent.
9. LexisNexis, http://w3.nexis.com/sources/scripts/info.pl?278252, accessed in
2010.
10. Eric D. Beinhocker, *The Origin of Wealth*, McKinsey & Company, New York,
2006, http://www.amazon.com/Origin-Wealth-byBeinhocker-Beinhocker/dp/
B006QXMAXU/.
11. U.S. Copyright Office, 2008, http://www.copyright.gov/circs/circ01.pdf.
12. Paul Romer, "Endogenous Technological Change," Working Paper 3210,
National Bureau of Economic Research (NBER), Cambridge, MA,
December 1989, http://www.nber.org/papers/w3210.pdf.
13. Yochai Benkler, *The Wealth of Networks*, Yale University Press, New Haven,
CT, 2006, p. 302.
14. Ibid., p. 303.
15. Richard Florida, "The Density of Innovation," September 22, 2010, http://
www.creativeclass.com/creative_class/2010/09/22/the-density-of-innovation/.

Epilogue

1. Michele Boldrin and David K. Levine, "James Watt: Monopolist," Mises
Institute, January 17, 2009, http://mises.org/daily/3280.
2. R. Buckminster Fuller, *Operating Manual for Spaceship Earth*, http://
en.wikipedia.org/wiki/Operating_Manual_for_Spaceship_Earth.
3. Heidi Ledford, "Supercomputer Sets Protein-Folding Record," *Nature*, October
14, 2010, http://www.nature.com/news/2010/101014/full/news.2010.541.html.
4. PEER 1 Hosting, http://www.peer1.com/.
5. http://babelverse.com/.
6. W. Daniel Hillis, *The Pattern on the Stone: The Simple Ideas That Make
Computers Work*, Basic Books, New York, http://www.amazon.com/
The-Pattern-On-Stone-Computers/dp/046502596X/.

ACKNOWLEDGMENTS

It took a crowd to make this book happen, and we are deeply grateful to all that have helped. We'd like to say a special thank you to a number of people, including Dan's wife Maya and daughter Tamara, who have been especially instrumental: Jouko Ahvenainen, Dara Albright, Giles Andrews, Casey Armstrong, Jennifer Ashkenazy, Roy Barak, Jason Best, W. Blanco, Fred Bryant, Zak Cassady-Dorion, Christian Catalini, Steve Cinelli, Amy Cortese, Brad Damphousse, Mat Dellorso, Kevin Dick, David Drake, Carl Esposti, Shane Fleenor, H. Flutto, Michael Fultz, Hadar Gafni, Andrea Gaggioli, David Geertz, Andrew Green, Kevin Berg Grell, Amir Gruber, Nate Hindman, Jessica Jackley, David R. Johnson, Jenny Kassan, Satish Kataria, Max Keiser, Karen Kerrigan, Karen Klein, Gijsbert Koren, Howard Leonhardt, Asaf Levi, Valto Loikkanen, Eric Mack, David Marlett, Brian Meece, Moshik Miller, Liran Nacker, Sherwood Neiss, Jane Palmieri, Mark Perlmutter, Douglas Rand, Steve Reaser, Danae Ringelmann, Slava Rubin, Orly Sade, Joshua Sams, Michael Shuman, Derek Slater, Paul Spinrad, Tom Stein, Josh Tetrick, Christopher Thomas, David Tomlinson, Brian Tsuchiya, Robert van Meer, Briana Viafora, Chris Ward, Joe Williams, Yishay Yafeh, Korstiaan Zandvliet, and so many, many others.

ABOUT THE AUTHORS

Kevin Lawton is a progenitor of PC virtualization, many-time start-up entrepreneur, trend-caster, and business/technical blogger. He contributes regularly to VentureBeat and SeekingAlpha.

Dan Marom is a researcher in finance and strategy at the Hebrew University of Jerusalem and a strategic consultant. More about him can be found at www.DanMarom.com.

INDEX